RIDDING CENTRAL AFRICA OF JOSEPH KONY: CONTINUING U.S. SUPPORT

HEARING

BEFORE THE

SUBCOMMITTEE ON AFRICA, GLOBAL HEALTH, GLOBAL HUMAN RIGHTS, AND INTERNATIONAL ORGANIZATIONS

OF THE

COMMITTEE ON FOREIGN AFFAIRS
HOUSE OF REPRESENTATIVES

ONE HUNDRED FOURTEENTH CONGRESS

FIRST SESSION

SEPTEMBER 30, 2015

Serial No. 114–99

Printed for the use of the Committee on Foreign Affairs

Available via the World Wide Web: http://www.foreignaffairs.house.gov/ or
http://www.gpo.gov/fdsys/

U.S. GOVERNMENT PUBLISHING OFFICE

96–818PDF   WASHINGTON : 2015

COMMITTEE ON FOREIGN AFFAIRS

EDWARD R. ROYCE, California, *Chairman*

CHRISTOPHER H. SMITH, New Jersey
ILEANA ROS-LEHTINEN, Florida
DANA ROHRABACHER, California
STEVE CHABOT, Ohio
JOE WILSON, South Carolina
MICHAEL T. McCAUL, Texas
TED POE, Texas
MATT SALMON, Arizona
DARRELL E. ISSA, California
TOM MARINO, Pennsylvania
JEFF DUNCAN, South Carolina
MO BROOKS, Alabama
PAUL COOK, California
RANDY K. WEBER SR., Texas
SCOTT PERRY, Pennsylvania
RON DeSANTIS, Florida
MARK MEADOWS, North Carolina
TED S. YOHO, Florida
CURT CLAWSON, Florida
SCOTT DesJARLAIS, Tennessee
REID J. RIBBLE, Wisconsin
DAVID A. TROTT, Michigan
LEE M. ZELDIN, New York
DANIEL DONOVAN, New York

ELIOT L. ENGEL, New York
BRAD SHERMAN, California
GREGORY W. MEEKS, New York
ALBIO SIRES, New Jersey
GERALD E. CONNOLLY, Virginia
THEODORE E. DEUTCH, Florida
BRIAN HIGGINS, New York
KAREN BASS, California
WILLIAM KEATING, Massachusetts
DAVID CICILLINE, Rhode Island
ALAN GRAYSON, Florida
AMI BERA, California
ALAN S. LOWENTHAL, California
GRACE MENG, New York
LOIS FRANKEL, Florida
TULSI GABBARD, Hawaii
JOAQUIN CASTRO, Texas
ROBIN L. KELLY, Illinois
BRENDAN F. BOYLE, Pennsylvania

AMY PORTER, *Chief of Staff*   THOMAS SHEEHY, *Staff Director*
JASON STEINBAUM, *Democratic Staff Director*

SUBCOMMITTEE ON AFRICA, GLOBAL HEALTH, GLOBAL HUMAN RIGHTS, AND INTERNATIONAL ORGANIZATIONS

CHRISTOPHER H. SMITH, New Jersey, *Chairman*

MARK MEADOWS, North Carolina
CURT CLAWSON, Florida
SCOTT DesJARLAIS, Tennessee
DANIEL DONOVAN, New York

KAREN BASS, California
DAVID CICILLINE, Rhode Island
AMI BERA, California

CONTENTS

RIDDING CENTRAL AFRICA OF JOSEPH KONY: CONTINUING U.S. SUPPORT

WEDNESDAY, SEPTEMBER 30, 2015

House of Representatives,
Subcommittee on Africa, Global Health,
Global Human Rights, and International Organizations,
Committee on Foreign Affairs,
Washington, DC.

The subcommittee met, pursuant to notice, at 2:06 p.m., in room 2172, Rayburn House Office Building, Hon. Christopher H. Smith (chairman of the subcommittee) presiding.

Mr. SMITH. The hearing will come to order. And good afternoon to everybody.

Since 1987, the Lord's Resistance Army, or LRA, has killed, raped, kidnapped, enslaved, or robbed thousands of people in the Great Lakes region of Africa and beyond. In October 2011, the Obama administration deployed about 100 military advisers to help Ugandan and other military forces in the region set out and capture or kill the members of a terrorist force that has now dwindled from thousands of fighters in late 1990s and early 2000s to fewer than 200 today, but remains a very real danger to people in the east and central regions of Africa.

This hearing will look at why the efforts to end the LRA are so critical for the international community and especially for the people who live in that region and how the United States counter-LRA program has worked so far.

Today's hearing is being held even in the absence of the Department of Defense or the State Department, whose relevant officials are unavailable for a few weeks—and we will invite them and do a second hearing with them—because it will serve as an acknowledgment of the importance of countering the LRA prior to the administration's decision on whether to continue the program. The decision of renewing the American deployment will come in the next few weeks. We trust the administration will decide to continue this worthy effort.

We hope to cover U.S. counter-LRA policy with administration witnesses, like I said. They have been invited, and we are just waiting for them to give us a date.

One can use a number of metaphors to describe the LRA today. It is like a wounded animal, less capable but still very dangerous. It is like a vulture, feeding off the existing misery it finds in countries otherwise troubled by conflict. The LRA is like a fire that is tamped down but not extinguished and can reignite at any time.

However, the danger posed by the LRA is not metaphorical. It is very real to those who still live in fear in eastern and central Africa and certainly to the hundreds of child soldiers whose lives have been harmed by its work.

The LRA is a vivid example of how ethnic strife can provide a cover for wanton viciousness. In the name of protecting the rights of Uganda's northern Acholi tribe, LRA founder Joseph Kony has brought only wretchedness to his people and their neighbors as well as the people living in surrounding countries. Efforts to come to a negotiated settlement have all come to naught because Kony apparently has no coherent demands. His terrorist group seems to want nothing more than chaos, murder, and destruction.

The international community has been much too quick to abandon humanitarian activities, largely because the number of victims has been reduced significantly. In confirmation hearings before the Senate Armed Services Committee last year, General David Rodriguez referred to the counter-LRA effort as ''a good success story,'' citing the group's decline and the American determination to support African officials to finish off the LRA.

Unfortunately, this is where the metaphors about the group must be kept in mind. Whenever the LRA has had a setback due to international efforts to eliminate it, the group's retaliation has been ruthless. Ongoing conflict in Central African Republic, South Sudan, and the eastern Democratic Republic of the Congo has provided a welcoming environment in which the LRA can hide and resume its deadly activities with less fear of regional government action against it. When you take your eyes off the LRA, they have enhanced maneuverability and opportunity to regroup.

Thanks to the #Kony2012 campaign by the advocacy group Invisible Children, who also paid a visit to my office in New Jersey, LRA became notorious worldwide and garnered international support, especially among the young, on behalf of a robust counter-LRA effort. Yet the staying power of social media is fleeting. There are always new causes, also legitimate and important, to draw attention away. Remember the ''Bring Back Our Girls'' campaign on behalf of the Chibok schoolgirls kidnapped by Boko Haram?

Our caring has to extend to the victims of the LRA and other such groups, which not only include those whom they attack but also those whom they cruelly use in their destructive campaigns. We have one such victim with us today, who can describe the ongoing desolation the LRA brings to so many young lives. We also have witnesses familiar and expert with the LRA and its terrorist activities, who will describe the ongoing threat that the group poses, however diminished their ranks may be.

Countering terrorist groups cannot depend on Twitter campaigns. The United States and other members of the international community must retain our resolve to capture and remove the leaders of the LRA and any terrorist group that threatens the lives and wellbeing of innocent people worldwide. Whether such groups pose a direct, confirmable threat to the homeland or not, by terrorizing those whom we help they oppose U.S. interests, and they must be dealt with.

I would like to yield to my good friend and colleague, Karen Bass, for any comments she might have.

Ms. BASS. Good afternoon, everyone.

Mr. Chairman, thank you for your leadership and for calling for today's hearing and the continuing U.S. support toward that effort.

This hearing offers us an opportunity to discuss the current state of affairs related to the movements and activities of the LRA and its notorious leader. My hope is that today's hearing will inform us of what the next steps are that the U.S. Government should take to help end the violence, kidnapping, and abuse that has been the standard practice of the LRA for decades.

I would also like to thank today's witnesses for agreeing to participate in the hearing, including regional experts from civil society, as well as Mrs. Thelin, who lost over two dozen members of her family in the Congo at the hands of members of the LRA.

I commend your dedication and commitment to working on this issue and helping to seek an end to the senseless violence that it produces. I look forward to hearing your testimony on the latest developments in the search for Kony as well as your insights into the devastation the LRA has wrought throughout central Africa and what can be done to stop it.

The Obama administration deployed close to 100 military advisers to Uganda in 2011 to help Ugandan and other military forces in the region to seek out and capture Kony and members of the LRA. The U.S. has also provided significant logistical support to Uganda's counter-LRA operations beyond its borders since 2008, while U.S.-based advocacy groups have contributed to U.S. policymakers' interest in the issue as well as public awareness among U.S. citizens.

While it is reported, as the chairman mentioned, that the numerical strength of the LRA has dwindled to maybe as small as 200 fighters today, their intimate knowledge of the inhospitable central African landscapes and total disregard for human life continues to make them a clear and present danger.

Though it originated in northern Uganda, the LRA now operates across a broad range of remote border regions between the CAR, the DRC, South Sudan, and even Sudan, according to reports. I don't know if people saw the Washington Post article today.

Mr. Chairman, did you mention that?

And there is also the concern as to maybe cooperation with Seleka, and maybe we will hear about that today.

Given the LRA's wide range of operations, I should also highlight the broad grouping of international bodies and actors involved in the effort to end the threat of this terrorist group. These include African governments, the U.N. political missions and peacekeeping operations, as well as the AU and the EU.

In 2012, the AU launched a regional task force against the LRA, which is led by Uganda, though it hasn't reached its full authorized troop strength of 5,000. And this is the kind of collaboration that is necessary to deal with and address the cross-border dimensions of the LRA activities.

In closing, I would like to encourage my colleagues in Congress and other U.S. Government agencies to sustain our effort to rid central Africa of Joseph Kony and to continue working with the international community to ensure that the LRA is no longer a threat to the innocent men, women, and helpless children it has preyed upon since its inception.

I am committed to joining you all in that effort and hope to learn from today's hearing how I can and we can be of greater assistance.

Mr. SMITH. Thank you very much, Ranking Member.

I would like to now introduce our three distinguished witnesses, who are expert and also extraordinarily brave in the work that they have done, and thank them for their leadership and for informing our subcommittee and, by extension, members of the full committee and the Congress by what you are able to convey to us, past and especially today as an update.

We will begin with Mr. Paul Ronan, who is co-founder of The Resolve LRA Crisis Initiative and currently serves as the project director. He also co-manages the LRA Crisis Tracker, a project that provides analysis of trends in LRA violence and activity to policymakers, humanitarians, and affected communities. He travels frequently to Uganda and LRA-affected areas in the CAR, DR Congo, and South Sudan. He also a frequent contributor to media outlets, congressional briefings, and think-tank fora. Prior to co-founding The Resolve, he worked at Caritas International and Franciscans International's U.N. advocacy office in New York.

We will then hear from Mr. Sasha Lezhnev, who is the associate director of policy at the Enough Project, where he focuses on peace, conflict, and corporate responsibility issues in central Africa. He is also founding director of the Grassroots Reconciliation Group, an organization that runs projects with former child soldiers in northern Uganda. He was based in Uganda for 2½ years as senior program officer with the Northern Uganda Peace Initiative and adviser to the chief mediator of the peace process with the Lord's Resistance Army. He is author of the book, "Crafting Peace: Strategies to Deal with Warlords in Collapsing States."

And, finally, we will hear from Ms. Francisca Mbikabele Thelin, who was born and raised in Dungu territory in the DR Congo. She was a founding teacher of Minzoto School. Though she moved away from the DR Congo in 1989, she travels to Dungu biannually. Because Francisca's family in the Dungu region has suffered profound losses of life during the LRA violence, her commitment to improving conditions in Dungu is strong and very personal. She founded the Friends of Minzoto in response to the dire conditions, extensive suffering, and pleas for help that she encountered in that region in 2010. She has made numerous public presentations on DRC history, culture, and the ongoing humanitarian crisis at universities, schools at every level, community, educational, and church events.

I would like to begin with Mr. Ronan.

And thank you again, all three, for being here.

STATEMENT OF MR. PAUL RONAN, CO–FOUNDER AND PROJECT DIRECTOR, THE RESOLVE LRA CRISIS INITIATIVE

Mr. RONAN. Chairman Smith, Ranking Member Bass, and members of the subcommittee, thank you very much for convening this timely discussion.

I would like to express my deep gratitude for the bipartisan leadership that this subcommittee and Congress as a whole, has shown in support of efforts to stop atrocities by the Lord's Resistance

Army, including the passage of the LRA Disarmament and Northern Uganda Recovery Act in May 2010.

I have been traveling to areas that have been affected by the LRA for 10 years now, and I have seen firsthand how the LRA Disarmament and Northern Uganda Recovery Act set into motion a significant strengthening of the U.S. Government commitment to resolve the crisis, including the deployment of 100 U.S. military advisers.

This support has greatly helped our African partners in the region to reduce the fighting capacity of the LRA by half from what it was in 2010, which was about 400. Kony now has fewer than 200 combatants left at his disposal, and this has greatly diminished the capacity of the LRA to commit atrocities. The graph up on the screen shows how the number of combatants has dropped. Killings by the LRA in eastern Central African Republic, northeastern Democratic Republic of the Congo, and western South Sudan have dropped dramatically, from 776 in 2010 to just 13 in 2014.

As encouraging as this progress has been, let there be no mistake: The LRA is not finished. Joseph Kony has outlasted three U.S. Presidents already, and, without renewed attention to this crisis, he will outlast both President Obama and the 114th Congress. His LRA forces have abducted over 400 Congolese civilians so far this year, which is more than they abducted in any of the previous 4 years. And this demonstrates clearly, I think, the danger that if U.S. and regional partners withdraw before removing Kony the LRA could quickly rebuild and resume mass atrocities.

The recent spike in attacks has also led to an increase in displacement and humanitarian needs, including in the areas where my colleague Francisca's family lives. And the next slide shows some of the trends there, including the uptick in abductions.

Still, with less than 200 fighters remaining, the LRA is at its weakest point in more than two decades, and Congress can continue to play a galvanizing role in ending LRA atrocities for good. The Resolve is supportive of House Resolution 394, introduced in July by a bipartisan coalition of 12 Representatives. The resolution outlines steps the administration should take to reinforce the counter-LRA strategy, including adjusting its priorities to put more emphasis on promising defection campaigns.

My recommendation is that within the next 6 months the U.S. military double, literally, the saturation level and geographic scope of the defection messaging targeting the LRA. You can see from the next slide, which is a map, just how vast the area that the LRA is operating in is.

We also urge Congress to ensure that the administration is adequately preparing for a post-Kony world. The LRA has long preyed on the communities that are marginalized by their own governments and face threats from other armed groups, and these challenges will remain long after Kony is finally brought to justice.

The sectarian conflicts that have left dozens killed or injured in Bangui and other areas of the Central African Republic over the past several days is a sobering reminder that the U.S. counter-LRA strategy must be part of a broader, long-term regional strategy that invests in strengthening fragile states and preventing mass atrocities.

USAID has invested in several innovative early recovery and civilian protection programs in LRA-affected areas, but most communities have been severely underserved by the U.S. and other donors. Too often, programming in these areas has been underfunded, delayed, and hampered by a lack of proper coordination. For the U.S. counter-LRA strategy to truly bear lasting fruit, USAID should invest in programs that spur longer-term economic recovery, reinforce community cohesion, and holistically reintegrate those who escape from the LRA.

In particular, I would like to reiterate that last point. I have interviewed dozens of men, women, and children who have risked rugged terrain, starvation, and Kony's wrath to escape the LRA. Most were abducted as kids. And each of their courageous attempts to reunite with their families is a testament to the strength of the human spirit. Still, many struggle to overcome the poverty, the medical problems, and the mental trauma inflicted by years in Kony's captivity. Helping those brave souls to reintegrate into their communities is equally, if not more, important than finally bringing Kony to justice.

Thank you for the opportunity to testify, and I look forward to your questions.

[The prepared statement of Mr. Ronan follows:]

Written Statement of Paul Ronan
Co-Founder and Project Director, The Resolve LRA Crisis Initiative

Before the House Foreign Affairs Committee Subcommittee on Africa, Global Health, Global
Human Rights, and International Organizations

Hearing: *Ridding Central Africa of Joseph Kony: Continuing U.S. Support*

September 30, 2015

Chairman Smith, Ranking Member Bass, and Members of the subcommittee, thank you for
convening this timely discussion. I would also like to express gratitude for the bipartisan
leadership this subcommittee, and Congress as a whole, has shown in support of efforts to
stop atrocities by the Lord's Resistance Army (LRA) rebel group. I am honored to be on this
panel with Sasha Lezhnev, a long-time advocate for a resolution to the LRA crisis, and
Francisca Thelin, whose expertise on this issue is matched only by the hospitality her
family has shown visitors to LRA-affected areas of Democratic Republic of Congo (Congo),
including myself.

I have been traveling to LRA-affected areas as part of my work with The Resolve LRA Crisis
Initiative since 2005, and returned from my most recent trip in July of 2015. I will focus my
comments on the trends in LRA activity and the US counter-LRA response since the passage
of the bipartisan *LRA Disarmament and Northern Uganda Recovery Act* in May 2010. In
particular, I wish to both affirm subsequent measures to address the crisis, and also draw
attention to how the Obama Administration and Congress can reinforce existing efforts to
bring LRA leader Joseph Kony to justice, demobilize remaining LRA fighters, and help
affected communities rebuild.

Progress following the passage of the LRA Disarmament Act
The LRA Disarmament Act was passed into law in the midst of one of the worst spikes of
LRA atrocities since Joseph Kony formed the rebel group in the late 1980s. Kony had 400
fighters at his disposal, and was actively training abducted children to expand his fighting
force. In the 18 months preceding the bill's passage, his LRA forces killed a staggering 2,300
civilians and abducted 2,650 more across a vast swath of territory encompassing parts of
the Central African Republic (CAR), Congo, and South Sudan.[1]

---

[1] LRA Crisis Tracker, statistic calculated September 24, 2015.

The 2010 LRA legislation, co-sponsored by a bipartisan coalition of 64 US Senators and 201 Representatives, required that President Obama deliver to Congress a comprehensive plan to deal with the LRA crisis. The White House boldly took up Congress' mandate, releasing an ambitious strategy that aimed to protect civilians, dismantle the LRA's command structure, encourage defections from the LRA, and assist affected communities. Its release had a catalyzing effect on the African Union (AU) and United Nations (UN), both of which subsequently issued counter-LRA strategies aimed at improving coordination among regional governments, UN peacekeeping missions, and humanitarian agencies active in LRA-affected areas.

In October 2011, President Obama revealed the flagship initiative of his counter-LRA strategy with the announcement that the US would deploy approximately 100 military advisers to assist regional forces authorized under the AU's counter-LRA Regional Task Force (RTF). In what became known as Operation Observant Compass (OOC), the US advisers have worked primarily with Ugandan forces, the most capable and equipped of the RTF contingents, deployed in eastern CAR. They have also trained national contingents from the CAR, Congo, and South Sudan, and collaborated with civil society actors on innovative "Come Home" defection campaigns using leaflets, radio messages, and aerial loudspeakers.[2]

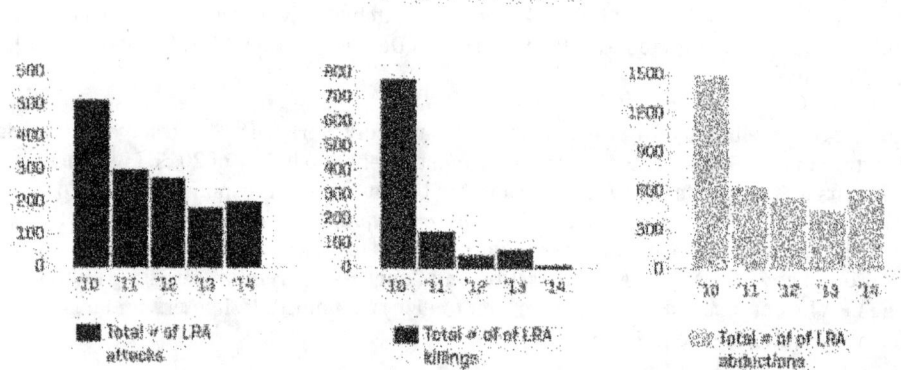

Trends in LRA violence

I would also like to highlight the work of field representatives from the State Department's Bureau of Conflict and Stabilization Operations.[3] They have not only played a critical role in fostering inter-agency cooperation within the Administration, but have also served as a key link between the US military and civil society groups on initiatives ranging from civilian early warning networks to Come Home defection campaigns.

---

[2] US State Department, "Fact Sheet: US Support to Regional Efforts to Counter the Lord's Resistance Army," 24 March 2014.

[3] Note: The LRA Crisis Tracker is the source of the data for all graphs and maps depicted in this statement.

Since the 2010 legislation was passed, combined counter-LRA initiatives have made significant progress against the rebel group. Mass child abductions have dropped dramatically and more than 350 women and children have escaped long-term captivity within the LRA.[4] The LRA killed 13 civilians in 2014, compared to 776 in 2010.[5] Several notorious commanders, including International Criminal Court-indictees Dominic Ongwen and Okot Odhiambo, have either defected or been killed. The total number of fighters at Kony's disposal has dropped from approximately 400 in 2010 to about 190 today.[6]

Several recent defections give us some hope that the LRA command structure, with Kony at its head, is eroding. When LRA commander Dominic Ongwen defected in December 2014, he did so with the assistance of fighters who defied Kony's orders not to allow him to escape. In May 2015, seven fighters who served as bodyguards to Kony or his inner circle defected and subsequently fended off several attempts by Kony loyalists to recapture them. Such a large defection of fighters from Kony's entourage is unprecedented in recent years.[7]

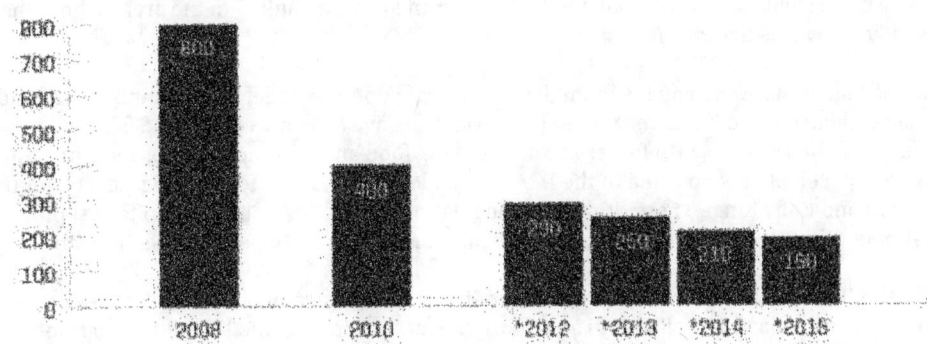

Estimated # of LRA combatants
(Ugandan and non-Ugandan)
*Estimated number of combatants as of 1 January

I had the opportunity to talk with several of these defectors in July. They told me that instead of simply defecting to the nearest town, they walked through remote forests and savannahs for an entire month to reach the US military base in eastern CAR. These young

---

[4] LRA Crisis Tracker, statistic calculated September 24, 2015.

[5] LRA Crisis Tracker, statistic calculated September 24, 2015.

[6] Paul Ronan, "The Kony Crossroads: President Obama's Chance to Define His Legacy on the LRA Crisis," The Resolve LRA Crisis Initiative, August 2015.

[7] Ronan, "The Kony Crossroads," August 2015.

men knew Kony would punish them severely if he caught them attempting to escape. Their daring is a clear sign that the US-supported defection campaigns are having a positive impact.

Remaining challenges

As encouraging as this progress has been, let there be no mistake: the LRA is not finished. As more fighters have left the LRA, those who remain have become more and more difficult to track down. Joseph Kony has outlasted three US presidents already, and without renewed attention to this crisis he will outlast both President Obama and the 114th Congress.

Kony still maintains significant control over a weakened but coherent command structure, and LRA groups still attack civilians across vast swaths of the CAR and Congo with little risk of being pursued. The number of LRA attacks and abductions has fluctuated considerably in recent years, indicating that counter-LRA efforts have not made irreversible progress in addressing the crisis. LRA forces have already abducted 417 Congolese civilians so far this year - more than they abducted in any of the previous four years.[8] This has led to an increase in civilian displacement and humanitarian needs, including in the areas where the family of my colleague Francisca lives.[9]

In the meantime, Kony and his immediate entourage operate largely from South Darfur and the neighboring Sudanese-controlled Kafia Kingi enclave.[10] As my colleague Sasha will explore in more detail, LRA forces are maintaining food and munitions stores by trafficking ivory from elephants poached in the LRA's Congolese safe havens to illicit markets in South Darfur and Kafia Kingi. These opportunistic relationships allow Kony's group to resupply without committing attacks that could give pursuing forces intelligence on their location.

US and Ugandan RTF forces face significant diplomatic constraints in accessing these safe havens, particularly in Kafia Kingi and South Darfur. In addition, the US military has not dedicated the appropriate mix of flexible, context-appropriate intelligence and airlift capabilities needed to pursue LRA commanders there. Though these challenges have been recognized and well-publicized for years, too often Administration officials have been slow to respond.[11] This has reduced the effectiveness of military operations – US and RTF forces have not had a significant battlefield victory against the LRA since June 2014 – and allowed senior LRA commanders to evade capture and minimize the flow of rank-and-file defectors.

---

[8] LRA Crisis Tracker, statistic calculated September 24, 2015.

[9] UN Office for the Coordination of Humanitarian Affairs (OCHA), "LRA Regional Update (January – March 2014)," 14 April 2014.

[10] Ronan, "The Kony Crossroads," August 2015.

[11] Paul Ronan and Michael Poffenberger, "Hidden in Plain Sight: Sudan's Harboring of the LRA in the Kafia Kingi Enclave, 2009- 2013," The Resolve, April 2013.

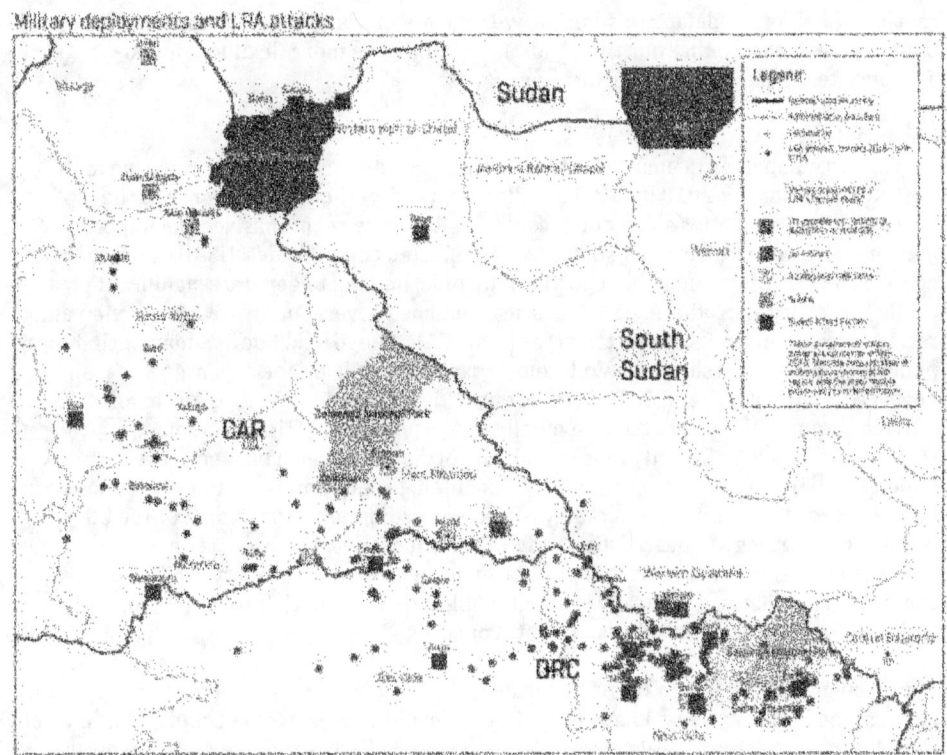

Military deployments and LRA attacks

Permanently ending LRA atrocities

The President and US Congress, along with the AU RTF and US troops working admirably in the theater of operations, deserve credit for reducing the LRA to a shadow of its former self. But renewed leadership is needed to move beyond mitigation of the crisis and achieve a definitive resolution. We cannot rest until Kony is captured, his command structure is dismantled, and the LRA no longer poses a significant threat to civilians.

A renewed effort to reach this goal must be centered on diplomatic and military initiatives that disrupt LRA safe havens in Kafia Kingi, South Darfur, and northeastern Congo. US advisers and their RTF partners must have consistent access to LRA safe havens, without which the counter-LRA effort cannot be successful. The US military must also adjust its priorities to put more emphasis on proven and promising defection campaigns. We recommend that within the next six months the US military double – literally – the saturation level and geographic scope of defection messaging targeting the LRA.

Congress can continue to play a galvanizing role in ending LRA atrocities for good. The Resolve is supportive of House Resolution 394, introduced in July by a bipartisan coalition of 14 Representatives. The resolution urges the President to reauthorize the deployment of US military advisers and expand efforts to bring Kony to justice and encourage his remaining fighters to defect. In addition, we urge members of the House to use the power of the purse to ensure that our troops on the ground have more flexible, context-appropriate intelligence and logistical resources.

Beyond Kony

We also urge Congress to ensure that the Administration is adequately preparing for a post-Kony world. The 2010 legislation called for a comprehensive response to the LRA crisis, and the President's subsequent counter-LRA strategy emphasized the importance of humanitarian and recovery assistance to LRA-affected communities. USAID and other US agencies have invested heavily in northern Uganda, helping to generate significant post-conflict recovery gains there. USAID has also launched several innovative protection and recovery programs in LRA-affected areas of the CAR, Congo, and South Sudan, including a public-private partnership with Vodacom to expand mobile phone coverage in northeastern Congo. The $300,000 project provided nearly 50,000 civilians in four LRA-affected communities with access to mobile phone networks.[12] However, most communities in LRA-affected areas outside of northern Uganda have been severely underserved by the US and other donors. Too often, programming in these areas has been underfunded, delayed, or hampered by a lack of coordination and vision. For the US counter-LRA strategy to bear lasting fruit, USAID must have the resources and leadership needed to invest in programs that spur longer-term economic recovery, reinforce community resilience, holistically reintegrate LRA escapees back into their communities, and address governance and human rights concerns.

In particular, I would like to reiterate the need for reintegration assistance to people who have escaped LRA captivity. I have interviewed dozens of men, women, and children who risked starvation, inhospitable terrain, and Kony's wrath to escape the LRA. Most were abducted as children, and each of their courageous attempts to reunite with their families is testament to the strength of the human spirit. Once they return home, most dedicate their energy to making up for lost schooling and pursuing livelihoods to support their families. Still, many struggle to overcome the poverty, medical problems, and mental trauma inflicted by years in captivity.[13] The international community has largely abandoned these brave souls, providing little or no support beyond what their families can give.

Conclusion

The LRA has long preyed on communities that are marginalized by their governments and vulnerable to violence from other armed groups. These challenges will remain long after Kony is finally brought to justice, but a decisive defeat of the LRA and boosted assistance to LRA returnees and affected communities would have a stabilizing effect and allow hundreds of thousands of people to return home. The successful execution of President Obama's counter-LRA strategy could also provide valuable lessons to his Atrocities

---

[12] USAID, "Cell Towers Strengthen Security in DRC: Mobile Phone Technology Increases Communication and Safety," July 2014.

[13] Dr. Emilie Medeiros, "Back but not home: supporting the reintegration of former LRA abductees into civilian life in Congo and South Sudan," Conciliation Resources, August 2014.

Prevention Board and future US Administrations about how strong interagency cooperation, investments in early warning mechanisms and community cohesion, and light-footprint military deployments can help prevent and respond to atrocities.

The alternative is more sobering. Should the fragile counter-LRA coalition disband and US and Ugandan RTF troops prematurely withdraw from LRA-affected areas, Kony's forces will continue to attack, abduct, and displace civilians across central Africa. Though Kony is integral to the LRA's current command structure, he eventually could seek to bestow authority on a younger generation of Ugandan LRA fighters that includes his sons and former bodyguards. If given the chance to rebuild, the LRA could metastasize: deepening ties with armed groups involved in illicit trafficking networks, further integrating non-Ugandan abductees into the officer ranks, and resuming mass atrocities.

Thank you again for the opportunity to testify about these issues. I look forward to your questions.

Mr. SMITH. Thank you so very much for that excellent testimony. And, without objection, your full statement, which had even more data and information, will be made a part of the record, as well as for all of our other witnesses.

We will now go to Mr. Lezhnev.

STATEMENT OF MR. SASHA LEZHNEV, ASSOCIATE DIRECTOR OF POLICY, ENOUGH PROJECT

Mr. LEZHNEV. Thank you so much. As someone who has spent the last 12 years interviewing and running projects for former LRA combatants, I really deeply appreciate your attention and continued vigilance on this very important issue, Chairman Smith, Ranking Member Bass, and Mr. Meadows and other members of this subcommittee and I really appreciate and thank you for the opportunity to testify on this important issue right at this critical juncture in the fight against the LRA.

From my years of working on the LRA, both with the Enough Project and in running projects for hundreds of former ex-combatants with the Grassroots Reconciliation Group, I have observed that the LRA is, frankly, one of the most resilient rebel groups on the planet in the face of adversity. It would win any ''Survivor'' competition.

Today, I am deeply concerned about the LRA's new trade in ivory and other commodities and its ability to regenerate itself going forward.

Strong bipartisan support in Congress to end the LRA's brutality has made a major impact, as Paul noted and as you noted in your opening statements, in improving human security and preventing atrocities in this war-torn region. Congress' LRA Disarmament and Northern Uganda Recovery Act as well as the Obama administration's deployment of U.S. military advisers to the African Union forces in 2011 have helped lead to a 90-percent decrease in LRA killings and a 30-percent decrease in attacks and have decimated its leadership.

When I started working in northern Uganda, over 1.8 million people were displaced, 90 percent of the population. Today, that number is down to 200,000. That is almost a 90-percent decrease, which is a huge impact on people's lives in that region.

But I am here to talk about how the LRA is not yet down and out, and, with a new trade in ivory, gold, and diamonds, it could make, in fact, a serious comeback, as it has done several times in the past.

Today, the LRA is increasingly poaching elephants for valuable tusks, trading that ivory for ammunition, supplies, and food in Sudan with the likely complicity of the Sudanese Government. This is actually the subject of last month's National Geographic magazine, where explorer Bryan Christy manufactured a fake ivory tusk and tracked it from LRA-held areas in Congo through to Sudan.

Critically, the LRA has a safe haven in Sudan-controlled territory Kafia Kingi. Joseph Kony has rarely left that area since 2011, and that is the chief area where the LRA trades ivory. Our team at Enough just spent a month in this area tracking the ivory trade and worked with the satellite company DigitalGlobe to help predict where the poaching might happen next, and here is what we found.

So, first of all, the elephants in Garamba National Park in Congo, which is a UNESCO World Heritage Site, are rapidly decreasing as a result of the poaching. From 20,000 elephants in the 1980s, there are fewer than 1,800 today. And this is a worrying, more global trend, with an estimated 35,000 elephants killed per year for tusks.

The LRA is one of the key armed groups responsible for poaching elephants in this area, along with Sudanese and South Sudanese poachers. There is one unit of LRA fighters that is permanently stationed in Garamba National Park under direct orders from Kony. And also under direct orders from Kony, including leadership from one of his sons, a second LRA unit then takes those ivory tusks to Sudan-controlled territories to trade them near a Sudan Armed Forces garrison in a place called Dafak, also in Kafia Kingi.

The main ivory trading town is called Songo. Sudanese forces have reportedly also provided valuable intelligence to the LRA, warning them of impending attacks. The ivory is then traded on by truck to Nyala, the capital of South Darfur in Sudan, and then likely to Khartoum for export to Asia.

Garamba National Park rangers say that if the LRA and other poachers are not stopped, the entire elephant population of that area could be wiped out.

Along with ivory, the LRA is also starting to trade in diamonds and gold. These resources give the LRA the ability to regroup and rearm. Looting and then trading in these items allows the LRA the opportunity to acquire food, ammunition, and other supplies. Over the past several months, LRA defectors that we have interviewed have come out with large amounts of fresh ammunition, along with rocket-propelled grenades.

You can trade 1 tusk for up to 25 boxes of bullets, and there are over 700 bullets in 1 box. It only takes one bullet to kill an elephant. This is critically important because the LRA already has weapons, both with its fighters and more guns buried in the ground, acquired from Sudan and from looting. So all it needs now are bullets, supplies, and Joseph Kony.

Kony is still in command and is central to the group despite the group's leadership decimation. With him in charge and with new ammunition, the LRA can abduct new fighters. And although overall LRA attacks are down significantly, as Paul pointed out, abduction numbers are up this year.

Now is the time to double-down on the U.S. counter-LRA mission and help end the LRA's horrific reign of atrocities against civilians once and for all. This could be done with a low-cost investment in a few key areas.

First, the Obama administration should reauthorize the U.S. advisers beyond October, the U.S. military advisers, with the primary goal of bringing Joseph Kony to justice. Simply managing or containing the problem will not stop Kony.

The U.S. mission should also provide additional airlift capacity to the AU forces and increase its efforts to get LRA fighters to defect from the group. I second Paul's recommendation on that. To that end, I urge you to sign on to House Resolution 394 on the LRA, a bipartisan resolution introduced by Representatives Jim McGovern and Joe Pitts.

Second, the United States should take a leading role in addressing Sudan's complicity in aiding the LRA. Sudan again denies that they are sheltering the LRA despite a wealth of evidence. I attach that evidence, compiled from the Enough Project, The Resolve, and Invisible Children, for the record with your permission.

Mr. SMITH. Without objection, it will be made a part.

Mr. LEZHNEV. Thank you.

The United States should deploy advisers close to the areas controlled by Sudan in Kafia Kingi so that it can gather precise intelligence on Kony's whereabouts.

Third, the United States should help shut down this blood ivory trade. To boost efforts on the ground, Congress should increase assistance to the Fish and Wildlife Service for antipoaching work in central Africa, for which it has experience. And the U.S. advisers on the counter-LRA mission should work more closely with the park rangers and help interdict the trade from Congo to Sudan, which is now a known route. You can go on the National Geographic Web site and find that exact route.

More broadly, the Obama administration's draft rules to help ban the ivory trade are an excellent step in the right direction, but they should also include only a small, de minimus provision for ivory sales, similar to what the State of New York has on the books for ivory laws.

I commend the many members of this subcommittee, including yourselves, for signing on to the Global Anti-Poaching Act, H.R. 2494, introduced by Chairman Ed Royce and Ranking Member Eliot Engel, and I urge other members of the subcommittee to do the same.

Finally, in the Fiscal Year 2016 appropriations process, Congress should not forget about the LRA and should continue to robustly support the counter-LRA operations. The U.S. Government deserves tremendous credit for sapping Kony's LRA of most of its strength and helping allow 1.6 million people to go home. However, the LRA has a history of regrouping, and we should not forget that. And so I am deeply concerned that its trade in ivory and other commodities could allow it to do so again. Now is not the time to pull the plug but, instead, to finish the job and bring Kony to justice.

Thank you, and I look forward to your questions.

[The prepared statement of Mr. Lezhnev follows:]

Testimony of Sasha Lezhnev
Associate Director of Policy, the Enough Project

House Foreign Affairs Committee
Subcommittee on Africa, Global Health, Global Human Rights, and International
Organizations

September 30, 2015

"Ridding Central Africa of Joseph Kony: Continuing U.S. Support"

Chairman Smith, Ranking Member Bass, and Members of the Subcommittee, thank you
for the opportunity to testify at this critical juncture in the fight against Joseph Kony's
Lord's Resistance Army (LRA) in central Africa.

From my 12 years of working on the LRA, both doing policy work with the Enough
Project and running projects for hundreds of former LRA combatants with the Grassroots
Reconciliation Group, I have observed that the LRA is one of the most resilient rebel
groups on the planet in the face of adversity. Despite 25 years of counter-insurgency
efforts mainly by Uganda, Kony's LRA lives on, as its fighters abduct children as young
as eight and move through dense jungles for thousands of miles on foot with virtually no
technology in some of the most remote terrain on the planet.

Today, I am deeply concerned about the LRA's new economic activities and its ability to
regenerate itself going forward.

Strong bipartisan support in Congress for ending the LRA's brutality has made a major
dent in improving human security and preventing atrocities. Following the passage of the
LRA Disarmament and Northern Uganda Recovery Act in 2010, which still today ranks
as the most popular standalone bill on Africa ever to pass Congress, the Obama
administration deployed approximately 100 Special Forces advisors to the African Union
Regional Task Force in October 2011. This has helped lead to a 90 percent decrease in
LRA killings and a 30 percent decrease in attacks,[1] and has significantly weakened a
group that has abducted more than 66,000 children and youths and is responsible for
more than 100,000 deaths over the past 28 years.[2] The number of displaced people as a
result of LRA attacks is down from 1.8 million to 200,000 today.[3]

The Problem

However, the LRA is not yet down and out, and with a new trade in ivory, gold, and
diamonds, it could make a serious comeback, as it has done in the past. Today, the LRA
is increasingly poaching elephants for valuable tusks, trading the ivory for ammunition,

supplies, and food in Sudan, with the likely complicity of the Sudanese government. This is the subject of September's *National Geographic* magazine, where explorer Bryan Christy manufactured a fake tusk and tracked it from LRA-held areas in Congo through to a town in central Sudan, Ed Daein.

The LRA is also starting to trade diamonds and gold in the Central African Republic, as documented by the Enough Project, Resolve, and Invisible Children through research in the field last fall and this past summer.

Critically, the LRA has a safe haven in Sudan-controlled territory, Kafia Kingi. Joseph Kony has rarely left that area since 2011, and that is the chief area where the LRA trades ivory.

Our team at Enough just spent a month in this area tracking the ivory trade, and worked with satellite company Digital Globe and the park rangers at African Parks in Congo's Garamba National Park last year to help predict where the poaching might happen next. Here's what we found:

- Elephants in Garamba National Park in Congo—a UNESCO World Heritage site—are rapidly decreasing as a result of poaching. From 20,000 elephants in the 1980s, there are fewer than 1,800 today.[4] This is a worrying more global trend, with an estimated 35,000 elephants killed per year for tusks.[5]
- Over 130 elephants were killed last year alone in Congo's Garamba National Park, and a 2-week killing spree in March of this year left 30 elephants dead.
- The LRA is one of the key armed groups responsible for poaching elephants in this area, along with other armed poachers from South Sudan and Sudan.
- One unit of LRA fighters is in charge of poaching elephants, under direct orders from Kony.
- A second LRA unit then takes the ivory tusks to Sudan-controlled areas to trade them near the Sudan Armed Forces garrison in Dafak, Kafia Kingi. The main ivory trading town is called Songo.
- The ivory is then traded on by truck to Nyala, the capital of South Darfur in Sudan, and then likely to Khartoum, Sudan's capital, mainly for export to Asia.
- Garamba park rangers say that if the LRA and other poachers are not stopped, the entire elephant population in the area could be wiped out.

Along with ivory, Kony has also issued orders to loot diamonds and gold. These resources give the LRA the ability to regroup and rearm. Looting and then trading these items allows the LRA the opportunity to acquire food, ammunition and other needed supplies. Over the past few months, LRA defectors have come out with fresh ammunition. You can trade one tusk for up to 25 boxes of bullets, and there are over 700 bullets in a box. It only takes one bullet to kill an elephant.

This is critically important because the LRA already has weapons both with its fighters and more guns buried in caches – acquired from Sudan and from looting over the past 20 years. So, all it needs now are bullets, supplies, and Joseph Kony. Kony is still in command and is central to the group. With him in charge and with new ammunition from the ivory trade, the LRA can abduct new fighters. Although overall LRA attacks and killings are down significantly since the U.S. advisors and African Union mission began in 2011, abduction numbers are up this year, nearly double what they were in 2014, according to the LRA Crisis Tracker.

The LRA also has the space to operate in the hinterlands of northeastern Congo, eastern Central African Republic, and Sudan-controlled territory in an area that U.S. military officers have called the "broccoli forest" because it's very difficult to see who is moving in the dense forests through the tops of the old growth trees.

The Solution

Now is the time to double down on the U.S. counter-LRA mission and help end the LRA's horrific reign of atrocities against civilians once and for all. This can be done with a low-cost investment in a few key areas.

1. First, the Obama administration should reauthorize the U.S. advisors beyond October with the primary goal of bringing Joseph Kony to justice. The U.S. assistance mission should also provide additional airlift capacity to the African Union forces and increase its efforts to get LRA fighters to defect from the group.

   To that end, I urge you to sign on to H.Res. 394, a bipartisan resolution introduced by Reps. Jim McGovern and Joe Pitts, which supports the U.S. mission and calls for an expansion of reintegration and anti-poaching programs.

2. Second, the United States needs to take the leading role in addressing Sudan's complicity in aiding the LRA. Two weeks ago, the African Union visited Khartoum to press it on the LRA, and Sudan officials again denied that they were sheltering the LRA, despite a wealth of evidence. I attach that evidence as part of the record, with your permission. The United States should deploy advisors close to the areas controlled by Sudan in Kafia Kingi so it can gather precise intelligence on Kony's whereabouts.

3. Third, the United States should help shut down the blood ivory trade. To boost efforts on the ground, Congress should increase assistance to the Fish and Wildlife Service for anti-poaching work in central Africa, which has experience in the region, and the U.S. advisors on the counter-LRA mission should work more closely with the park rangers and help interdict the trade from Congo to Sudan. More broadly, the Obama administration's draft rules to help ban the ivory trade are an excellent step in the right direction, but they should only include a small *de minimus* provision for ivory sales, similar to the State of New York's ivory laws.

   I commend the many members of the Subcommittee for signing on to the Global Anti-Poaching Act, H.R. 2494, introduced by Chairman Ed Royce and Ranking

Member Eliot Engel, and urge other members of this Subcommittee to do the same.

4. Finally, in the FY16 appropriations process Congress should continue to robustly support the counter-LRA operations.

In sum, the U.S. government deserves tremendous credit for sapping Kony's LRA of most of its strength and helping allow 1.6 million people to return to their homes. However, the LRA has a history of regrouping, and I am deeply concerned that its trade in ivory and other commodities could allow it to do so again. Now is not the time to pull back, but instead to finish the job and bring Kony to justice.

Thank you, Chairman Smith and Ranking Member Bass for continuing to pay attention to this critical human security problem. I look forward to your questions.

---

[1] The Enough Project took figures for documented monthly attacks and killings by the Lord's Resistance Army from the LRA Crisis Tracker, which has recorded data from December 2007 to the present. Enough calculated the average figures for LRA attacks and killings from both before (December 2007 to November 2011) and after the U.S. advisors deployed (December 2011 to June 2015). We found a total of 1,219 LRA attacks (an average of 25.4 per month) before U.S. advisors deployed and a total of 767 attacks (an average of 17.84 per month) after the deployment. We found a total of 2,979 documented killings (an average of 62.06 per month) before deployment and a total of 151 documented killings (an average of 3.51 per month) after deployment. Our calculations for the difference in average monthly attack rates before and after deployment: 25.4 - 17.84 / 25.4 = 0.297, or a 30 percent decrease. Our calculations for the difference in average monthly killing rates before and after deployment: 62.06 - 3.51 / 62.06 = 0.943, or a 94 percent decrease. When we removed LRA attack and killings figures from December 2008 and January 2009 from our calculations—to control for violence rates associated with a significant counter-LRA operation—our re-calculated rates indicated monthly average attack rates were 25.5 and the average monthly killing rates were 44.7—the latter a significant decrease from the unadjusted figure of 62.06. Recalculating with these figures, we again found attacks fell by 30 percent and average monthly killing rates fell by 92 percent. Our adjusted calculations for attacks: 25.5 - 17.84 / 25.5 = 0.300, or a 30 percent decrease. Our adjusted calculations for killings: 3.51 - 44.7 / 44.7 = 0.921, or a 92 percent decrease. Spreadsheets with calculations are on file with the Enough Project and available upon request. Data available from LRA Crisis Tracker at http://lracrisistracker.com/ (last accessed July 2015). For news reporting indicating that the U.S. advisors authorized by President Obama in October 2011 deployed in October and November 2011 see Jake Tapper and Luis Martinez, "Obama Sends 100 US Troops to Uganda to Help Combat Lord's Resistance Army," ABC News, October 14, 2011, available at http://abcnews.go.com/blogs/politics/2011/10/obama-sends-100-us-troops-to-uganda-to-combat-lords-resistance-army/. For reports surrounding the December 2008 counter-LRA operation see Jeffrey Gettleman and Eric Schmitt, "U.S. Aided a Failed Plan to Rout Ugandan Rebels," *The New York Times*, February 6, 2009, available at http://www.nytimes.com/2009/02/07/world/africa/07congo.html?pagewanted=all&_r=1&; Grace Matsiko, Paul Amoru, and Risdel Kasasira, "UPDF attacks Kony," *Daily Monitor*, December 15, 2008, available at http://www.monitor.co.ug/News/Education/-/688336/761130/-/10grmo/-/index.html.

[2] Evidence from a 2006 study by the Survey for War Affected Youth (SWAY) estimates that at least 66,000 youths between the ages of 14 and 30 were abducted. A U.N. report estimates that the LRA is responsible for more than 100,000 deaths. Jeannie Annan, Christopher Blattman, and Roger Horton, "The State of Youth and Youth Protection in Northern Uganda: Findings from the Survey for War Affected Youth," p. 55

(Survey of War Affected Youth, September 2006) available at
http://www.chrisblattman.com/documents/policy/sway/SWAY.Phase1.FinalReport.pdf; U.N. Security
Council, "Report of the Secretary-General on the activities of the United Nations Regional Office for
Central Africa and on the Lord's Resistance Army-affected areas," S/2013/297, para. 68, May 20, 2013,
available at http://www.un.org/en/ga/search/view_doc.asp?symbol=S/2013/297.
[3] UN OCHA, "LRA Regional Update: Central African Republic, DR Congo and South Sudan (April - June
2015), available at http://reliefweb.int/sites/reliefweb.int/files/resources/LRA_Regional_Update_Q2-2015-
20150722.pdf
[4] Enough Project, Digital Globe, and African Parks, "Poachers without Borders: New Satellite Imaging and
Predictive Mapping to Empower Park Rangers and Combat Ivory Traffickers in Garamba National Park,"
January 28, 2015, available at http://www.enoughproject.org/files/PoachersWithoutBorders_28Jan2015.pdf
Ed Mazza, "Elephant Massacre Uncovered In Democratic Republic of Congo; 30 Animals Killed In 15
Days," *Huffington Post* (March 26, 2015), available at
http://www.huffingtonpost.com/2015/03/26/elephant-massacre-congo_n_6945266.html
[5] According to the Wildlife Conservation Society. For more information, see http://www.wcs.org/elephants/

Mr. SMITH. Thank you very much, Mr. Lezhnev, for your testimony.

I would like to now ask Ms. Thelin if she would proceed.

STATEMENT OF MS. FRANCISCA MBIKABELE THELIN, FOUNDER AND PRESIDENT, FRIENDS OF MINZOTO

Ms. THELIN. Thank you. My name is Francisca Thelin. I want to sincerely thank the chairman, ranking member, and the entire subcommittee for this opportunity to speak today on behalf of those suffering from the violence of the LRA, the Lord's Resistance Army.

Though I have lived in the United States for 26 years and am a U.S. citizen, I grew up in the Dungu territory in the Democratic Republic of the Congo, a region deeply affected by the violence of Joseph Kony and the LRA. I am the founder of a small nonprofit called the Friends of Minzoto, which supports local community efforts in the Dungu area to recover from the LRA violence.

My dear friend Lisa Shannon authored a book entitled, ''Mama Koko and the Hundred Gunmen,'' which tells my family's story of experiencing the LRA crisis firsthand. Since 2008, 28 members of my family have been murdered by the LRA. Most were chopped with the machete, many in front of their loved ones. Six children in my family were abducted and forced to become LRA's sex slaves or child soldiers. Although one eventually escaped, he came home so psychologically damaged that he is a danger to our other children and cannot live at home. We can only assume that the others who have not returned home have died.

At the age of 69, my mother spent months at a time hiding in the bush with no blankets or supplies, taking care of multiple babies and teenagers, and getting sick with pneumonia before coming back home to nothing. The LRA had looted everything.

For 5 years, my family and every family in the Dungu territory lived in total terror because of the LRA. Unable to go to the fields to grow their crops, everyone was hungry. Many who did not die at the hand of the LRA died of starvation and malnutrition.

Even now, the situation is not fully back to normal. Thousands of internally displaced families that took refuge in the Dungu years ago still live there with no land of their own, barely surviving day to day. Many of them live in meager homes next to the river, the only place where they could settle, and they are regularly flooded out of their homes when the rains come.

Life for them is so difficult, but they are afraid to go home to their villages—and with good reason. Many of those who did go back to their villages were killed, or many are still being forced to give all their crops and their belongings to the LRA when they attack.

When I was in Dungu in 2010 interviewing survivors of the LRA, I would ask them, what do you want from the U.S. Government? Their answers were always the same: We want peace, we want Kony out. I promised to share their message with my Government in the United States, but I wasn't sure exactly how I would do that. Today, I am finally able to deliver on that promise, and I am very grateful for this opportunity.

So I am here today to ask you, Honorable Members, in the strongest possible terms to continue to support the African Union and the U.S. advisers in their efforts to end LRA violence. Please do not allow this mission to lose strength until the LRA is stopped and Joseph Kony and his leaders have been held accountable for their horrific crimes.

Why is continued support from the U.S. so important when the LRA threat seems diminished? LRA attacks are still taking place. Particularly in the Congo, abductions by the LRA have increased over the past year, which further traumatizes the population. In the minds of the communities, the LRA rules the bush. But the bush is our bank; it is where we find food, where we clear land to cultivate our crops in order to feed our families and to earn livelihoods.

I have story after story of my connection to people attacked by the LRA, but it would take days to tell them all, and they are very painful to share.

As I close, I want to emphasize that these communities targeted by the LRA are severely neglected. They do not have resources on their own to get rid of the LRA. And they have suffered long enough. The commitment of the U.S. is critical to their survival and to lasting peace. Please, do not give up before the crisis is actually over.

I am speaking for all Congolese enduring LRA violence when I thank you for all that the U.S. Government has already done to help bring this crisis to an end. In light of how far we have come and how precious these lives are, I urge you and every Member of Congress to stay committed to seeing LRA violence finally ended.

Specifically, I ask you to support House Resolution 394, which reinforces the U.S. Government's commitment to ending LRA violence. Secondly, I urge you to provide funding in the U.S. budget that would support the local recovery initiatives in the LRA-affected communities. And, lastly, I ask you to use your position of influence to press Congo's Government to promote a free and fair election on time. I ask you to use your help to make sure that the communities like Dungu do not continue to be so marginalized and vulnerable to groups like LRA in the future.

I want to thank you again for your care for families, like my own, who have suffered from this crisis. And I thank you for this opportunity to fulfill my promise to them and to represent their voices here in Washington.

Thank you.

[The prepared statement of Ms. Thelin follows:]

Statement of Francisca Thelin
Founder, Friends of Minzoto

At the House Foreign Affairs Committee Subcommittee on Africa, Global Health, Global
Human Rights, and International Organizations Hearing: *Ridding Central Africa of
Joseph Kony: Continuing U.S. Support*

September 30, 2015

My name is Francisca Thelin. I want to sincerely thank the Chairman, Ranking Member,
and the entire Subcommittee for this opportunity to speak today on behalf of those
suffering from the violence of the Lord's Resistance Army, or LRA.

Though I have lived in the United States for 26 years and am a U.S. citizen, I grew up in
Dungu Territory in Democratic Republic of Congo, a region deeply affected by the
violence of Joseph Kony and the LRA. I am the founder of a small non-profit called
Friends of Minzoto, which supports local community efforts in the Dungu area to recover
from LRA violence. My dear friend, Lisa Shannon, authored a book entitled *Mama Koko
and the Hundred Gunmen,* which tells my family's story of experiencing the LRA crisis
firsthand.

Since 2008, 28 members of my family have been murdered by the LRA. Most were
chopped with machetes; many in front of their own loved ones. Six children in my family
were abducted and forced to become LRA sex slaves or child soldiers. Although one
eventually escaped, he came home so psychologically damaged that he is a danger to
our other children and cannot live at home. We can only assume that the others, who
have not returned home, have died.

At age 69, my mother spent months at a time hiding in the bush with no blankets or
supplies, taking care of multiple babies and teenagers, and getting sick with pneumonia,
before coming back home to nothing. The LRA had looted everything.

For five years, my family -- and every family in Dungu Territory -- lived in total terror
because of the LRA; unable to go to their fields to grow their crops. Everyone was
hungry. Many who didn't die at the hands of the LRA died of starvation and malnutrition.
Even now, the situation is not fully back to normal. Thousands of internally displaced
families that took refuge in Dungu years ago still live there, with no land of their own,
barely surviving day-to-day. Many of them live in meager homes next to the river, the
only place where they could settle, and they are regularly flooded out of their homes

when the rains come. Life for them is so difficult, but they are afraid to go home to their villages, and with good reason. Many of those who did go back to their villages were killed, or many are still being forced to give all of their crops and belongings to the LRA when they attack.

When I was in Dungu in 2010, interviewing survivors of the LRA, I would ask them, "What do you want from the U.S. government?" Their answer was always the same: *we want peace. We want Kony out!* I promised to share their message with my government in the United States, but I wasn't sure exactly how I would do that.

Today, I am finally able to deliver on that promise. And I am very grateful for this opportunity. So I am here today to ask you honorable members, in the strongest possible terms, to continue to support the African Union and the U.S. advisors in their efforts to end LRA violence. Please do not allow this mission to lose strength until the LRA is stopped, and Joseph Kony and his leaders have been held accountable for their horrific crimes.

Why is continued support from the U.S. so important when the LRA threat seems diminished? LRA attacks are still taking place. Particularly in Congo, abductions by the LRA have increased over the past year, which further traumatizes the population. In the minds of the communities, the LRA rule the bush. But the bush is our bank. It is where we find food, where we clear land to cultivate our crops in order to feed our families and to earn a livelihood.

I have story after story of my connections to people attacked by the LRA, but it would take days to tell them all, and they are very painful to share. As I close, I want to emphasize that these communities targeted by the LRA are severely neglected. They do not have the resources on their own to get rid of the LRA, and they have suffered long enough. The commitment of the U.S. is critical to their survival and to lasting peace.

Please do not give up before the crisis is actually over. I am speaking for all Congolese enduring LRA violence when I thank you for all that the U.S. government has already done to help bring this crisis to an end. In light of how far we have come, and how precious these lives are, I urge you and every member of Congress to stay committed to seeing LRA violence finally ended. Specifically, I ask you to support House Resolution 394, which reinforces the U.S. government's commitment to ending LRA violence. Secondly, I urge you to provide funding in the U.S. budget that will support local recovery initiatives in LRA-affected communities; and lastly, I ask you to use your positions of influence to help promote free and fair elections in Congo. This is necessary to help make sure that communities like Dungu do not continue to be so marginalized and vulnerable to groups like the LRA in the future.

I want to thank you again for your care for families like my own who have suffered from this crisis, and thank you for this opportunity to fulfill my promise to them and represent their voices here in Washington.

———————

Mr. SMITH. Ms. Thelin, thank you so very much for your testimony.

We do have two votes on the floor, but we don't have to be there just yet, although in a moment or so. But we will take a brief recess and then come back.

I would like to ask just a couple of opening questions.

Ms. Thelin, your nonprofit supports recovery efforts for the victims of the LRA. What are the greatest needs? Are individuals, especially children and women, getting the psychological help that they need after being traumatized? Is the faith community stepping up, whether it be Christian or Muslim, to meet those needs, in your opinion?

Ms. THELIN. Actually, I cannot really tell you that there is something happening to help them now. But it was in 2010 when I was there, there was a group helping them, and it seems like they are struggling now with funds, funding. They don't have the money to continue. But there is nothing really at present.

Mr. SMITH. All right. I appreciate it.

Would either of our other witnesses like to comment on the psychological component of helping those who have been traumatized?

Yes, Mr. Ronan.

Mr. RONAN. That is a great question. And I think that the answer is that very little support is now available to the people that escape the LRA.

Many of them might receive maybe a few days, when they first come out, of some basic medical treatment or some counseling. But, over the long term, the children and the women and especially the adult men who do escape, all of whom were abducted as kids, receive very little support.

And that is, I think, a problem that will be manifested and will continue for years in the future if these people are not able to properly reintegrate into their communities.

Mr. SMITH. Thank you.

Mr. LEZHNEV. I would just add, if I may, the scars of war, of being a child soldier don't disappear overnight. And, unfortunately, many NGOs and organizations have pulled out of northern Uganda because there is no longer active conflict happening there, and that is an area of tremendous need.

The organization that I helped found, the Grassroots Reconciliation Group, runs a psychosocial trauma counseling project for roughly 700 ex-combatants and their families, but it is really a drop in the bucket when you think that the LRA has abducted some 66,000 youth. And if you have spent 5 or 10 or 15 years in the bush, constantly being forced to kill your friends and your family members, those psychological traumas will not go away overnight.

So there is a lot more need for assistance in that area. And our groups are putting together a letter exactly on this issue now. We will be happy to send it to you.

Mr. SMITH. Okay.

Let me just ask you, Mr. Lezhnev. You make a very ominous warning that it could make a serious comeback, as it has done in the past. In my opening comments, I tried to emphasize that, and I know Ranking Member Bass feels the same way.

Is there any belief or any expectation that the administration will not continue this vital program, again, which all three of you have wholeheartedly embraced and endorsed?

Mr. LEZHNEV. I think that there is still a debate happening within the administration between those who really want to see the job finished and those who say, well, the leadership is decimated, attacks are down, the capacity is lowered, let's just contain the problem and move on to other priority areas.

Mr. SMITH. Is it because of cost? I mean, what is the reason?

Mr. LEZHNEV. I think part of it is cost. Part of it are the growing crises in South Sudan and CAR, other priority areas.

But, from our experience, as long as Kony is there, he is very skillful at getting new resources and surviving and moving to territories where he has a safe haven. So, as long as he is there, we need to continue working.

Mr. SMITH. The committee will stand in brief recess, subject to the call of the chair. And I thank you. And sorry for this delay.

[Recess.]

Mr. SMITH. The subcommittee will resume its sitting. And, again, I apologize for that delay. Just a few additional questions. And I know Karen is on her way back, as well as Mark Meadows.

Mr. Ronan, in your testimony, you talked about the Come Home defection campaign and how important that is. You make a point that I found very interesting. You talked about how some of the people, defectors, had walked for an entire month to reach the U.S. military base in eastern CAR.

And I am wondering, is it because it is that dangerous to go anywhere else other than to the U.S. forces? And how is it that they knew where they were? A month of walking can take you many hundreds of miles. And I am just wondering if you could elaborate on that.

Mr. RONAN. Yes. And thank you very much. That is, again, a very good question.

And I think that, first of all, it is just important to reiterate the ability that Kony has to instill propaganda into the combatants in his force, which he has an advantage of, of course, because many of them were abducted when they were very young. So the starting point to try to convince these combatants to defect from the LRA is very difficult. It is very difficult to do that.

So I really do think it is a testament to the ingenuity and the hard work of the U.S. advisers and the civil society partners that they work with that they have been able to devise messaging, whether it be by FM radio, by speakers that are strapped onto helicopters, or by leaflets, to really penetrate the propaganda that Kony tries to instill.

And this most recent case from a few months ago, when these seven bodyguards to Kony who were operating near the Sudanese-controlled areas of the Kafia Kingi enclave with Kony, when I interviewed them after they had defected, they said that it was a result of this messaging that they had received that has been supported by the U.S. military that they knew that they could safely defect to where the U.S. base was. And they knew where the U.S. base was as a result of that messaging.

So for me, to talk to these guys who had been abducted 15 years ago when they were very, very young and hear them talk about how the U.S. base was in many ways a beacon for them that they were trying to reach, and then they did reach there, and they were received and were able to return to their families, again, was just a powerful reminder that these defection campaigns can really have a positive impact.

Mr. SMITH. Let me just ask you—all of you, if you would like to speak to it, but you have testified that the U.S. Government has not dedicated the appropriate mix of flexible context-appropriate intelligence and airlift capabilities to pursue the LRA. And given the heavily forested areas in which they operate, why do you think this strategy has developed, and what impact has it had on the success of the counter-LRA program?

And I would just note parenthetically that in Vietnam, there was the defoliant Agent Orange; obviously, it caused many of our servicemembers and Vietnamese to become very, very sick. I used to chair the Veterans' Affairs Committee, and the number of illnesses attributable to that are huge.

But, since then, we have developed—and I have been to military bases where this technology is being deployed and actually affixed to helicopters—the look-down capability which is enormous for the U.S. military. Are we using that kind of capability? The ability to see through foliage is enormous, and I am wondering if that is being deployed, as far as you know.

Mr. RONAN. I would say that to recognize the challenges that the U.S. advisers in the field are dealing with, the LRA is now really composed of 200 combatants that are spread over an area the size of California. So you don't want to underestimate how difficult it is to find them in this area.

At the same time, I do think that the U.S. could do a better job of ensuring that the helicopters and the ISR assets that are deployed out to these regions are appropriate to how the LRA operates. And I think that that is why it is very important that the U.S. continue to try to make sure that these assets and personnel are deployed in areas near the Kafia Kingi enclave and where Kony himself is operating.

As far as the specific technology that is being used now, unfortunately, I don't know exactly what that is. I don't have access to that. But I would say that we have seen a very positive trend in what the advisers have been doing over the past year or so of really trying to talk to as many people as they can and to develop human intelligence. Because the LRA is interacting with many people in these areas, whether they are trying to sell ivory or acquire food, and that intelligence has led to actionable operations in the past that have been very successful. So that is an alternative approach that I think can be very useful.

Mr. SMITH. Thank you.

Mr. LEZHNEV. I would just also add that I think that the location issue that Paul highlighted is very important, because, for a while, U.S. advisers were deployed in an area of southeastern CAR that was pretty far away, frankly, from a lot of the LRA operating areas, so Kafia Kingi in northeastern Congo. We are learning that the U.S. advisers are moving closer to the LRA areas of operation now, which is good. That is something we have been advocating for, frankly.

And it is difficult to operate in those areas. I mean, these are areas with no roads at all. It takes quite a bit of capacity from airlift to actually get there.

I think that the defection issue and location of defection areas is another important consideration that the U.S. advisers and the Obama administration could put some more effort into, in terms of providing some more of these locations for LRA fighters to defect, right? They shouldn't have to walk for 400 miles to get there, because that really is the safest area. There have been LRA people, LRA members who have been lynched in certain areas, as communities are afraid of the fighters.

So I think there could be some more efforts there, but most of the attacks are happening now in northeastern Congo, so there is a need there, in particular.

Mr. SMITH. Ms. Thelin, you said that the communities now feel that the LRA rule the bush. And I am wondering how this has impacted the relocation of villagers. Are people combining settlements or moving to what they perceive are safer zones?

Ms. THELIN. In general, people who are in the town of Dungu, they are safer than the people who live in the villages. Because the LRA have changed their strategies now. They come publicly by the side road and captured people. And then they take two and hold two back. If they capture four of them, then they hold the two, and they give the two others money, send them to the market to buy food for them and bring it to the bush in order to release all the group. And they give them an ultimatum: Go to the market, buy food, bring it to us, and we will release all of you, or we kill all of you now. And they do as they are told, and they go buy food, they bring it. Once they bring it, then they will release them.

So they don't live far from the road, and now they are not scared. And I think they playing a mind game, just the way they started. At the beginning, they were in the market, people were thinking, oh, they are nice, they are just looking for a place to settle and they are not bothering us. And then the attacks started. And now the feeling is that they are getting very strong and powerful. They have money. They have everything.

According to people who escaped them—it was in July when my brother, who works for the early warning radio system—so his group went to this village. So he was sick that day, didn't go with them, but that group was captured by the LRA. And then they hold two of them, send two to the market to Dungu. So they come, and they noticed the authorities of what was happening. They said, okay, the group was captured by the LRA, they send us to the market, we are buying food, we are taking it back to them so in order to release the rest of the group who were there. And then they did, they took the food back.

So when they were there, they see that the LRA have everything. They have a solar panel, they have a radio, they have machine guns, they have enough food, a lot of money. And they released them after 2 days, and they come home.

So now is that the feel is that pretty soon the attacks will start again.

Mr. SMITH. We have all read this morning's front-page Washington Post story, and I am just wondering if you might want to comment. A very provocative headline: "U.S. Troops Have Turned to Some Unsavory Partners to Help Find Warlord Joseph Kony."

And the article talks about how U.S. forces have begun working closely with Muslim rebels, known as Seleka, who toppled the central government 2 years ago. And then it goes on. One official described the group as the mafia.

And yet, as you read on, the answer from National Security Council spokesman Peter Boogaard is that U.S. forces do not provide intelligence or operational assistance to Seleka factions or other armed groups, though he acknowledged that our military advisers may meet with actors who have information on LRA activities.

I would appreciate your comments on the article, because I know you have all read it. The $5 million that have been offered by State, have there been any takers or anything close to someone providing actionable information about what could be done?

And, again, if I could again circle back to your testimony, Mr. Ronan, when you said that 417 Congolese civilians so far this year have been abducted, more than they abducted in any of the previous 4 years, as if there might be a shift in their modus operandi, what happens to those abductees?

And then the 200 that we keep talking about that are still Kony's killers, who are they? Are they child soldiers now grown up? If you could give us a sense, a profile of who we think they are, at least, it would be very helpful. All three of you.

Mr. LEZHNEV. I will just start off with the first question. You asked a lot of questions at the same time, Mr. Smith, but that is perfectly fine.

So, with regard to the Seleka Washington Post article, quite frankly, I think this is very misleading. First of all, U.S. forces need to be operating in that area, which is close to where Kony is located and, clearly, they need to communicate with any authorities or forces in that area, former Seleka commanders. Seleka is no longer an active force itself. There are former Seleka commanders who are in control of that area.

This is not an Islamist, a jihadist group. They are not establishing Sharia law or anything like that. They have been in control of that area for roughly 10 years. So if anyone wants to move in and out of that area, they, of course, have to communicate to them.

We have talked to our folks on the ground in that area. We do not have any knowledge that the U.S. has provided any financial assistance to the Seleka. We would obviously strongly condemn the U.S. providing any assistance, financial assistance, to those rebels, but we do not have any information.

And, again, we think it is very important for the U.S. to be present in areas close to where Kony is. Otherwise, we will continue circling around here for another decade with this mission.

Mr. RONAN. I would just like to reiterate everything from what Sasha just said. You know, I think that the Washington Post article did outline, you know, some of the challenges that U.S. forces in the region face, but an Islamist group that they are partnering with is not one of them. I think that the terminology that was used there was just inaccurate.

As has been said, what the U.S. troops are doing is they are talking to people who have knowledge about where Kony and his fighters may be. They are not doing that in exchange for material support or for doing joint operations or anything like that.

And, as I said before, I think that the human intelligence piece of this operation is something that we should be praising and not something that we should be overly concerned about in the way that was represented in that article.

The one thing that I will add on to that is I do think that it is important for the State Department and the U.S. to clarify is that whatever conversations are happening between the U.S. military and these former Seleka, to make sure that those conversations are being coordinated with the response to the broader conflict in the CAR, which, as we have noted, has gotten much, much worse in the past few days. Again, we can't see the LRA as in a vacuum. It is very much interconnected with what is happening in the broader region.

On the question of the patterns of LRA abductions in the DRC, in Congo, fortunately, what we have seen over the past few years is, with the pressure that the U.S. and Ugandan troops are putting on the LRA, Kony doesn't really have the capacity to do the mass child abductions and train them to join the LRA. We have seen a few cases of that, but a vast majority of the people that have been abducted over the past few years are adults, who are used to carry goods from their community into the bush for the use of the LRA, and then they are released.

And I don't want to understate or say that that is not important. Even being abducted for a few days is very traumatic. And the people in these areas often have not very many goods. So if you take their farming tools and their harvest and their seeds, then that can be really a terrible thing.

And, as far as the 200 combatants left within the LRA, most of them, over 100, are Ugandans who were abducted as kids and are now adults. So they have really grown up within the LRA. And then maybe another 30 to 50 of them would be Congolese, South Sudanese, or central Africans who have been abducted in the past 4 or 5 years and may be a bit younger.

Mr. SMITH. The U.S. armed services that are deployed there, have there been any injuries, fatalities, years to date?

Mr. RONAN. Not that I am aware of, no.

Mr. SMITH. I have other questions, but I will yield to my good friend Ms. Bass and then come back.

Ms. BASS. Thank you.

Once again, thank you all for your testimony and taking the time out today to speak with us.

I wanted to ask several questions. I wanted to follow up on a question that the chairman asked that I don't think you guys responded to, and that is the $5 million.

So I wanted to know, first of all, earlier this year, one of the LRA commanders was surrendered, captured—a little bit of difference there in terms of how people view it. What happened? Because if he surrendered or was captured, did anybody contribute to that? Is the $5 million still there? That is such a huge amount of money, it is hard for me to understand why that isn't enough to generate his capture.

Mr. RONAN. So, as far as Dominic Ongwen, who was a senior LRA commander indicted by the ICC in 2005, in late 2014, Kony basically put him under arrest within the LRA and indicated that he was going to kill him. So Dominic Ongwen, with the help of some other fighters within the LRA, was able to escape.

And then, as you said, the sequence of events after that is a bit fuzzy, about whether he was captured or whether he surrendered. He was certainly trying to surrender. And he came into the custody of some former Seleka, who got in touch with the U.S. military in the town of Obo. And it is unclear if these former Seleka were even aware of who he was and the reward that they may have been eligible for, but they transferred him to the custody of the U.S. military. He was then taken to The Hague.

So, again, to our knowledge, the $5 million, no part of that has been disbursed for Dominic's arrest or his capture.

One of the challenges that I think that we have seen, talking to the U.S. military as they have tried to implement this plan, is that many people in the region don't believe it. And it is not because the $5 million is too little; it is because that is such a huge number that many people simply think that it is a trick. So, I think that there is a learning process that needs to happen about how to advertise this in a way that will incentivize people to contribute.

Ms. BASS. I can actually understand that.

Ms. Thelin, could you respond to that question? I mean, if $5 million is so much that it seems a trick—and I could kind of understand that, because it sounds like trillions—should it would be done differently?

And so your thoughts, too, on two things: One, why that hasn't delivered Kony; and then, two, in response to what Mr. Ronan was saying, does it need to be done differently? Is it a smaller amount? Outreach? How is it done?

Ms. THELIN. Well, thank you for your question, but that is not in my expertise.

Ms. BASS. Oh, no, no. Well, but I am asking you that from the perspective of you being from the area and given your past and continued relationship with the people, the culture, the community, the ties. That is why I am asking you.

Ms. THELIN. So, first of all, I didn't know anything about the money.

Ms. BASS. You didn't know about the $5 million?

Ms. THELIN. I didn't know about the money.

Ms. BASS. Oh, boy.

Ms. THELIN. And, second of all, people are really thankful for when the African Union troops got there, they were so happy, and with the U.S. advisers, and the things were going very good. And the people actually started staying outside. They feel like there is life coming back.

But they still wonder why it is taking too long to capture Kony. You have done all these things; U.S. advisers are there, the African troops are there. But in the town of Dungu itself, life is okay, but it is overpopulated because everybody in the villages moved into the town, who used to be only for 20,000 people, but now I don't know the number, but I feel like the roads are packed. They are just thinking that it is taking too long to capture Kony.

Ms. BASS. Well, that is pretty dramatic for me to hear that you were not aware of it, considering you are active in the area. So maybe there is something that needs to be examined in terms of how we are getting the word out there.

I wonder, Mr. Lezhnev, what happens the day after we capture Kony? I worry sometimes that our focus—and, obviously, I would like to see him captured. But, you know, with Boko Haram, with al-Qaeda, with the Taliban, I mean, we have captured leaders before, only to have them replaced the next day.

So, given that the LRA has really been reduced in size, do we know anything about intelligence, second-line leadership, what would happen the day after we captured Kony?

Mr. LEZHNEV. It is a great question. I think it is one that we have all been debating and talking about for several years.

Frankly, the rest of the LRA's leadership is very much decimated according to what it used to be. There were several commanders who were there from the late 1980s and early 1990s. They have all either been killed, defected, or are awaiting trial in The Hague.

The ones who are rising up in the leadership now are Kony's sons, who are young, 21, 23, 24. They are not—I do not think they have the capacity to lead this type of rebellion.

I have spoken to so many ex-combatants who speak about Kony's ability and spiritual powers, and that is why they follow him. And they believe those spiritual powers. And he has, of course, manipulated his control of information so that he knows when something is going to happen, and so that will appear to someone locally as him having powers.

But in terms of what would happen after we would capture or kill Kony, I think that there would probably be a couple of LRA groups who would try to operate in the local areas. But if they knew that Kony was not there backing them up, giving them orders, resupplying them with arms, ammunition, food, medicine, et cetera, you know, the defections would increase pretty dramatically.

I don't think that the U.S. should give up then, that that should be the end of our program. I think that there need to be programs—recovery programs, rehabilitation programs, psychological programs like we talked about earlier, which are very important to help rebuild those areas. We are trying to get a specific road funded out in that area, which really hamstrings movement throughout that whole region. So that——

Ms. BASS. Who are you trying to get——

Mr. LEZHNEV. I would want to say something one other thing with regard to the $5 million.

Ms. BASS. No. Who are you trying to get the fund the road?

Mr. LEZHNEV. Well, the U.N., African Union——

Ms. BASS. So go ahead about——

Mr. LEZHNEV [continuing]. World Bank.

Ms. BASS [continuing]. The $5 million.

Mr. LEZHNEV. So, with the $5 million, one interesting thing that we uncovered in our new interviews with ex-combatants is that, for the first time in our lifetime of working on the LRA, there has been a serious attempt on Joseph Kony's life, that his bodyguards actually tried to kill him. They failed, and so, therefore, they ran very quickly away. But, you know, that speaks to some of the pressure.

It is really too bad that many local communities are not aware of this $5 million reward, and so we obviously need to do a much better job at communicating that and also communicate it in local terms. But several of the military folks in LRA, they are aware of it.

And, also, I think that helps Kony stick in an area that is pretty depopulated. There is, of course, the possibility and many rumors circulating that he would go to south Darfur, which would be further in Sudanese territory, et cetera. The fact that he is not moving in there, I think, is largely a result of this $5 million, because people are more aware there, and they would like to get that money. And that is a much more populated area.

Ms. BASS. Did the bodyguards escape? You said they ran away. Did they escape?

Mr. LEZHNEV. They defected, yeah.

Ms. BASS. They did?

Mr. LEZHNEV. Uh-huh.

Ms. BASS. Do you know if there is any effort to involve them in the search for him?

Mr. LEZHNEV. Absolutely. Yeah.

Do you want to talk about that?

Mr. RONAN. Yeah. Just to add that these same defectors that tried to kill Kony were the ones that I was talking about before. When they did escape, they made a beeline for the U.S. base, because they knew that that was a place where they——

Ms. BASS. I see.

Mr. RONAN [continuing]. Could safely go. And as a result of intelligence that they gave to the U.S. and the Ugandan troops, there was an arms cache and some food stores that were destroyed on the central African side of the border with Sudan.

Ms. BASS. You know, you mentioned at the beginning—I am not sure which one; it might have been you, Mr. Ronan—about the gold and diamonds, I think. Where is that coming from? Is that coming from the DRC? How are they lined up to get that? I understand the poaching; that is obvious.

Mr. LEZHNEV. So it is mostly looting in the Central African Republic. That area is pretty well known for its gold and diamond mines. Of course, CAR diamonds are some of the most famous in the world for their quality.

The defectors that we interviewed talked about Kony having jars of gold nuggets and, sort of, a half-liter bottle of diamonds waiting to sell for the right time. There were some rumors that he was going to buy anti-personnel land mines to encircle him so that no one could attack his positions. That, of course, doesn't work very well if you have helicopters and so forth, but anyways.

So, yeah, it is mostly looting and from artisanal mining. They have not set up, as far as we know, more complex conflict-minerals type of operations where they actually operate mines. Not yet.

Ms. BASS. Thank you.

And, Ms. Thelin, you might have mentioned this earlier before I returned, but could you talk about your organization, the work your organization does? And then do you receive any support from the U.S. Government?

Ms. THELIN. Well, my organization is very small. I can call it just a baby organization. So I got my 501(c)(3) in December 2014. And basically I started working at a school. I give them nice, clean water. They dig a well and put a pump. And then now we are in the process of building latrines and handwashing stations.

And, also, I have big ambitions, but I don't know where the money would come from. But it will happen someday.

Ms. BASS. It is okay. What are the ambitions? Ambitions first, money second.

Ms. THELIN. So I want to help because to have a good community, that means a healthy community. So if we want to be really good, like, we need strong people, good health, so they need clean water. And I have to build some 60 more wells and build latrines. Now they don't have public latrines. And we have many people, and it is really not good, the sanitation is not good.

And also I need, like, some kind of equipment for the hospital. We have a big hospital, it is an original hospital. But the only thing, when I visited this January, the only equipment that was there was a 60-year-old microscope and a refrigerator with vaccines. So people with broken legs and all kinds of critical conditions, they take the bus and go on this nightmarish road, dusty road, to Goma or to Bunia to get the treatment. They don't have x-ray, MRI, or any kind of salt. And that is my ambition.

So, this summer, I made some Congolese food and some barbecue in my backyard to raise money for latrines, and I did well. I think I did a little over $10,000.

Ms. BASS. That is great from a barbecue.

Ms. THELIN. Some people of goodwill helped me. They were just so passionate about my speech and what my community is going through, and they helped, and now that latrine is in the process.

Ms. BASS. Great. Thank you. Thank you very much.

Thank you, Mr. Chair.

Mr. SMITH. Thank you very much, Ms. Bass.

Let me just ask you, Mr. Lezhnev. You have reminded us of the terrible toll that the LRA has imposed upon innocent people—the abduction of more than 66,000 children, 100,000 deaths over the past 28 years. And then you talked about the displaced, down from 1.8 million to 200,000 today.

200,000 is an enormous number of people displaced, and I am wondering if you can tell us, maybe break that out a little bit further—who they are, where they are, how they are faring, and the prospects, if there are any, in the near term, intermediate term for return.

And then you also, in talking about the blood ivory trade, point out that—and I thought this was amazing, sadly, tragic—that you can trade one tusk from an elephant for up to 25 boxes of bullets. And there are over 700 bullets in a box. That comes out to 17,500 bullets. That is a lot of ammo. And you have talked about how Kony seems to have more resources like more ammo recently.

Who is buying the ivory, and how much of that clientele might be Americans?

Mr. LEZHNEV. I will answer the ivory question first, and I will defer to Paul on the displacement figures.

With regard to the ivory, we are heavily investigating that. It is pretty difficult to access the Kafia Kingi area because it is controlled by Sudan, and they don't like to allow visas for people like us on the panel to access that area. But, nevertheless, we are doing our best to investigate it, and particularly with LRA defectors who were involved in the ivory trade.

I interviewed one of the big LRA ivory traders a few months ago. There are a couple of buyers that are based in Sudan. There are some merchants in this town called Songo. We are told that there are some Sudan Armed Forces commanders who were also buying the ivory. They obviously have the bullets. The LRA is also needing food and medical supplies and so forth, so the local merchants will supply those. And then it mainly gets traded to Asia.

So there is a lot more effort needed in terms of helping law enforcement inspect ports. And that trade is likely going from Port Sudan on to places like Dubai and then onward to China, and so there is a need to help the customs and border patrol and law enforcement in those areas to intercept those containers.

Frankly, right now, it is pretty difficult to identify which containers they are, but we started a new initiative at Enough called The Sentry, and The Sentry is really conducting these investigations into the financing of conflicts. So we hope to come with new information about this, about which containers need to be intercepted and which traders need to be sanctioned.

Mr. RONAN. And on the issue of displacement, I want to thank you, actually, for how you framed that. Because I think many times people say, oh, there has been a drop from 1.8 million to 200,000, and that is not very many. And you are absolutely right to point out that is an enormous amount of people. And, in fact, the vast majority of them are Congolese and live right in the areas near where Francisca is from.

And I would also like to say that there are some analysts that actually think that that 200,000 number is quite a bit higher.

And just to reiterate, the reason why many people are displaced, even if the number of attacks has gone down, is because the memory of the massacres that the LRA did in 2008, 2009, and 2010, they are never going to leave the memories of the people that had to witness them. So, even if the LRA is not as violent as it once was, the legacy that they have really has a ripple effect that will keep people displaced as long as Kony is free.

I would also like to point out that, in these same areas where a majority of displaced people live in Congo are, due to a drop in funding from the donor community, there has been a withdrawal of 16 of the 19 international humanitarian groups that had been providing much-needed food, water, and sanitation. Many of the groups that were operational there have had to withdraw, and it is not because there is a decrease in the number of people that need the services.

And, of course, I have seen, myself, the incredible work that the Congolese themselves are doing in trying to address these needs, but there is a need for renewed international funding, as well.

Mr. SMITH. The African Union forces that are being advised by the 100 Americans deployed there, could you maybe give us some insights that might be unique to your experiences about who they are, how well they are doing, how many are there? What kind of capabilities do they have, like airlifts, or is that all ours? I am just wondering how robust of an effort is that by the AU.

Mr. RONAN. Yeah. Thanks.

On the question of the AURTF and the troops that are deployed out there, again, I want to recognize the bravery of many of those soldiers, who are often not very well-equipped and are tasked with walking through some dangerous, dangerous jungles in order to find dangerous people.

Now, that said, it is unfortunate that I have to report that none of the countries that have dedicated troops to the AU force to track the LRA have been able to fulfill the obligations that they signed up for.

And this, again, brings back the issue of regional instability, where in South Sudan and in the Central African Republic we have seen, you know, massive problems that have prevented those governments——

Mr. SMITH. How far short have they been?

Mr. RONAN. I believe that the Ugandan Army has come the closest. They have around 1,000 troops, I believe, is the number that they said that they have dedicated, which is about half of what they were committed for. And the Ugandan troops are really doing the bulk of these operations. They are the ones that we can largely attribute the decrease in the number of combatants to.

The South Sudanese and the central Africans really have hundreds, if not dozens, of troops that they have been able to dedicate, which is far, far lower than what they had said.

There has been a ray of hope, I think, with the U.S. advisers working with the very small number of Congolese troops that have been doing operations in and around Garamba Park, which is where the LRA gets much of its ivory. So that hasn't provided much success yet, but I think it is a positive step.

Mr. SMITH. Can I just ask you, should the administration phase out or terminate the U.S. deployment, what impact would that have on the Ugandans and others in terms of their commitment to troops?

Mr. LEZHNEV. It would have a devastating and debilitating impact.

Paul and I were witness to the solely Ugandan-led operations for many years in northern Uganda and further. Frankly, although, overall, over many years, it was a war of attrition and LRA numbers slowly went down, there were so many botched operations, many times when the Ugandans supposedly wouldn't have the fuel for a helicopter to go and chase Kony. A third of the Ugandan Army were listed as ghost soldiers during that time.

So the intelligence collection, the efforts to pursue Kony, the decimation of their leadership—again, four of the five top commanders are no longer in action—those are results of successful operations that the U.S. has helped really coordinate and really improve the capacity. So if the U.S. advisers were to go away, I think we would definitely see a resurgence in the LRA.

Mr. SMITH. A very timely caution. And we will convey that to the administration immediately and take your words, if you don't mind, backed up by our observations. And I am sure Karen and I and others on the committee will want to put into a letter immediately that kind of question, because that would be devastating.

I would like to yield to Sheila Jackson Lee, the gentlelady from Texas.

Ms. JACKSON LEE. Mr. Chairman, forgive me for rushing in and rushing out. I want to thank you for your courtesies. I am not a member of the committee, and you have always extended to me a courtesy.

Forgive me. The loud phone that was ringing was calling me to the floor, so I apologize.

I want to thank Ms. Bass, as well, for always being gracious. This is a passion of mine, the continent. And these issues of conflict, we have worked on these for a number of years. So I want to thank you for your leadership and the leadership of this subcommittee.

I will be asking cross-examination questions, and I thank you for indulging me on these.

It looks as if Mr. Kony has been here since the beginning of civilization. It looks like it has been so long that my frustration level has gone—now you are telling me that his children—and if we are here and blessed by life and you come back and tell me his grandchildren, then I know that we are—not that you are doing something—that we haven't done what we needed to do.

So if I might draw something to the chairman's attention, and I want to submit into the record—and please note that I am going to make the connection, as we do sometimes in the courtroom in a prosecution case. But I want to note, Mr. Chairman, the speech of President Buhari of Nigeria before the United Nations, and I want to commend some language very quickly.

I would ask unanimous consent if I might put this in the record.

Mr. SMITH. Without objection, so ordered.

Ms. JACKSON LEE. He speaks about peace. He talks about the sustainable efforts of the United Nations. And he says, Nigeria has contributed to U.N. peacekeeping efforts in Ethiopia, Liberia, Sierra Leone, et cetera, just to reflect upon what they have done in the past.

Then he goes on to say that "[p]eace . . . is close to the hearts of Nigerians, as we are in the front line in the war on terror. Boko Haram's war against the people of Nigeria, Chad, Niger, and Cameroon may not attract as much worldwide attention as the wars in the Middle East" but the people are suffering.

"This war is about values between progress and chaos; between democracy and the rule of law. Boko Haram celebrates violence against the weak and the innocent and deplorably, they hide behind their perverted interpretation of Islam. Boko Haram is as far away from Islam as anyone can think of."

So I make the nexus to—first, I want to congratulate the newly-elected President, Mr. Buhari. We met with him in Nigeria, and he made a commitment that he was going to end the siege of Boko Haram by the end of 2015.

So I raise these questions about the involvement—first, my number-one question is—and let me mind my manners and thank all of the witnesses.

And, particularly, Ms. Thelin, thank you for your passion. And, of course, $10,000, as you well know, the story of the fishes and loaves—you may know it; it is in the Christian faith—which means you get a little bit and then it multiplies. And we look forward to seeing your work multiply.

But my question is to you. And I again want to offer sympathy to Ms. Thelin for losing over two dozen of your family members, and I think sometimes we tend to forget that.

But on this issue of Mr. Kony, who is now passing his legacy on, I have several questions. One, where is the African Union in this, and where are the surrounding nations? I know, obviously, in central Africa, he is surrounded by Uganda, Rwanda. But where is the African Union, as its ability under its charter to utilize troops in this instance?

The other is on the question of the gold, the diamonds, and, obviously, the ivory. What role do American consumers, purchasers, individuals like the dentist who went to Zimbabwe almost as I was there and that unfortunately saw the demise of Cecil the lion—but what role do we play in that?

And have you any comment on the—or let me say that I thank them, but I just want to know what the comment might be as the U.S. special operations are pointedly working and have drawn together some unique characters as their collaborators under the African Command.

I happen to be a strong supporter of AFRICOM, because it was under our watch a couple years ago that we fought for AFRICOM—in this instance, the Foreign Affairs Committee and the Congressional Black Caucus. And I think they play a vital role for peace in Africa.

So I see you taking notes, so I will yield on those questions. And I know that you will, in your answers, as you did to the chairman, say what we can do. But I don't think I can hear one more moment that the grandchildren now have taken over from Kony without us bringing this to an end.

Let me thank you very much.

Ms. THELIN. So I would have to say that, when the African Union got to Dungu, everybody—I received a lot of calls from my family that everybody was happy that their presence was there at that time, because in 4 years that was the first time people could be outside of the compound in the morning, early morning or in the evening, the hours that mostly LRA was supposed to attack.

And, also, when U.S. special advisers came, everything seems to be nice. But, again, it just looks like they are not pursuing Kony, and it is taking too long. Because even though the presence is there, the LRA are still abducting people. They will come past the United Nations compound—I don't know how—and in a few meters from the compound and abduct people in the light, bright light day, and attack and killing.

So people sometimes are so disappointed that, okay, America is a superpower, so if really they decided to capture Kony, they would do so in no time, but it is taking too long. But they are thankful that you are doing what you are doing already, and they are hoping that he will be captured some time soon.

Ms. JACKSON LEE. Thank you, ma'am. And I would only say to you that, when we have our U.S. special ops on the ground, you can be assured they are focused and pointed, and maybe sometimes unseen, but purposely functioning.

I hope that the chairman—I heard his question before, but I would like to find a way to get a further answer from the African Union—not from you; I heard what you said—for their enhanced work. They may be at the limits of what they can do. And with that collaboration, the African Union of course doing what they are doing and the limits of what we can do with our particular guidelines of use on the continent, I can assure you that the special ops of the United States military, particularly AFRICOM there, that they are focused. But I thank you.

You two gentlemen, if you could take a stab at the other two, and I will listen as I have to run to the floor. But thank you so very much.

Thank you, madam, very much for that answer.

Ms. THELIN. Thank you.

Mr. LEZHNEV. Thank you so much for your questions.

Just regarding the ivory and the gold and the diamonds, most ivory goes to China for consumption there, but there is still some that comes here. And so Congress' efforts to combat wildlife trafficking are very important. And the new Obama administration draft regulations that are starting to put in place a ban on the ivory trade in the United States are very important.

The Fish and Wildlife Service came out recently with a de minimis exception for some very limited ivory trade, for example, in bows of violins and cellos and those kind of things. There is a danger that if you allow that de minimis exception to be too high that, in fact, that would be a major loophole, and we would not want that. You can break a tusk into 100 pieces——

Ms. JACKSON LEE. Yeah.

Mr. LEZHNEV [continuing]. Or 1,000 pieces, you know, that doesn't make the trade any less valuable.

So what we really need to do is cut that trade down and make sure that that de minimus exception is very low. So any efforts from Congress to weigh in with the administration on that issue would be more than welcome.

New York State already has that de minimus exception. California is also passing a law on this, waiting for the Governor's signature.

So with regard to pressing China on this issue.

Ms. JACKSON LEE. Yeah.

Mr. LEZHNEV. We were very happy to see the President pressing the Chinese President just last week on the ivory, and they did come out with a pretty strong statement on that. But that needs followup. This is a pretty lucrative business out there.

With regard to gold and diamonds, gold is still a commodity that is used for money laundering, terrorist financing. There was a recent FATF report which talked about gold and money laundering in use by various rebel groups around the world, including in Congo. And, in particular, there are some conflict traders out there that need to be the focus of investigations and targeted sanctions.

We, ourselves, are investigating some of those in the Middle East at the moment and will be happy to provide the subcommittee with more information on that as we get it. We are writing a report and have some whistleblowers within some of these organizations that are trading the conflict gold.

I will let Paul answer, though.

Ms. JACKSON LEE. Thank you very much. Thank you.

Mr. RONAN. On the AU involvement, I think that the African Union's approach to counter the LRA was unique, in the sense that the force that they have deployed is an AU-authorized force and not an AU-mandated force. And that distinction has basically meant that the AU itself is providing very little support to the Ugandan, the South Sudanese, the Central African, and the Congolese troops that are out there. So it is really up to the countries themselves to equip their troops, which would be different than how most AU and U.N. peacekeeping operations work.

And, unfortunately, if the LRA is operating in your country, it is the canary in the coal mine. It is not the reason why your country is allowing a group like this to operate, but it is taking advantage of that.

So, by leaving it up to the countries themselves to provide all of the support to their troops, we are left where we are now, which is that the Ugandans are really the only force out there that is capable of really pursuing the LRA, and even their capacity has been very, very limited.

So I think that this has revealed some of the weaknesses from an AU and an international perspective as far as how they approach this and reinforces the need to make sure that we have adequate troops there and that they have the equipment that they need to actually pursue the LRA in an effective manner.

Ms. JACKSON LEE. Mr. Chairman, thank you very much.

Thank you so much. You have given me work to do.

Thank you so very much, Mr. Chairman, for your kindness.

Mr. SMITH. Thank you. We are glad to have you.

That concludes the hearing. I, first of all, want to just thank you on behalf of the subcommittee for your testimonies and your leadership. It is a privilege to receive expert testimony from such highly informed, highly motivated, and wise leaders. We really benefit greatly. The people who are suffering will benefit from this, as they have already by your leadership.

And we will contact the administration; I know that is why we did it now, to get your insights right now so that they make the right decision, which I believe they will do, to keep this important program going.

So anything you want to ever add within the period of time for this hearing but also on the issue itself, particularly as it relates to the other countries. The members of this subcommittee, including the chairman and Greg Simpkins, our staff director, and other members of the staff, we are in constant contact with the leaders of these countries and if there is something we need to convey to any of these other people, please let us know, and we can bring that word to them, again, from such experts.

The hearing is adjourned.

[Whereupon, at 4:05 p.m., the subcommittee was adjourned.]

APPENDIX

SUBCOMMITTEE HEARING NOTICE
COMMITTEE ON FOREIGN AFFAIRS
U.S. HOUSE OF REPRESENTATIVES
WASHINGTON, DC 20515-6128

Subcommittee on Africa, Global Health, Global Human Rights, and International Organizations
Christopher H. Smith (R-NJ), Chairman

September 30, 2015

TO: MEMBERS OF THE COMMITTEE ON FOREIGN AFFAIRS

You are respectfully requested to attend an OPEN hearing of the Committee on Foreign Affairs, to be held by the Subcommittee on Africa, Global Health, Global Human Rights, and International Organizations in Room 2172 of the Rayburn House Office Building (and available live on the Committee website at http://www.ForeignAffairs.house.gov):

DATE: Wednesday, September 30, 2015

TIME: 2:00 p.m.

SUBJECT: Ridding Central Africa of Joseph Kony: Continuing U.S. Support

WITNESSES: Mr. Paul Ronan
Co-Founder and Project Director
The Resolve LRA Crisis Initiative

Mr. Sasha Lezhnev
Associate Director of Policy
Enough Project

Ms. Francisca Mbikabele Thelin
Founder and President
Friends of Minzoto

By Direction of the Chairman

The Committee on Foreign Affairs seeks to make its facilities accessible to persons with disabilities. If you are in need of special accommodations, please call 202/225-5021 at least four business days in advance of the event, whenever practicable. Questions with regard to special accommodations in general (including availability of Committee materials in alternative formats and assistive listening devices) may be directed to the Committee.

COMMITTEE ON FOREIGN AFFAIRS

MINUTES OF SUBCOMMITTEE ON _Africa, Global Health, Global Human Rights, and International Organizations_ HEARING

Day _Wednesday_ Date _September 30, 2015_ Room _2172 Rayburn HOB_

Starting Time _2:05 p.m._ Ending Time _4:05 p.m._

Recesses | _1_ | (_2:44_ to _3:08_) (____to ____) (____to ____) (____to ____) (____to ____) (____to ____)

Presiding Member(s)

Rep. Chris Smith

Check all of the following that apply:

Open Session ☑ Electronically Recorded (taped) ☑
Executive (closed) Session ☐ Stenographic Record ☑
Televised ☑

TITLE OF HEARING:

Ridding Central Africa of Joseph Kony: Continuing U.S. Support

---

SUBCOMMITTEE MEMBERS PRESENT:

Rep. Karen Bass, Rep. Mark Meadows

NON-SUBCOMMITTEE MEMBERS PRESENT: _(Mark with an * if they are not members of full committee.)_

Rep. Sheila Jackson Lee*

HEARING WITNESSES: Same as meeting notice attached? Yes ☑ No ☐
(If "no", please list below and include title, agency, department, or organization.)

STATEMENTS FOR THE RECORD: _(List any statements submitted for the record.)_

Evidence of the LRA's Presence in Sudan-controlled territory, submitted for the record by Mr. Mr. Sasha Lezhnev
Nigerian President Buhari's Speech to the U.N. General Assembly, submitted for the record by Rep. Sheila Jackson Lee

---

TIME SCHEDULED TO RECONVENE _____
or
TIME ADJOURNED _4:05 p.m._

Gregory B. Simpkins
Subcommittee Staff Director

MATERIAL SUBMITTED FOR THE RECORD BY MR. SASHA LEZHNEV, ASSOCIATE DIRECTOR OF POLICY, ENOUGH PROJECT

Annex 1: Evidence of the LRA's Presence in Sudan-controlled territory from 2009-present

Enough Project

September 30, 2015

The Lord's Resistance Army (LRA) has been present in Sudan and Sudanese-controlled territory since 2009 and continues to be present in these areas today, particularly the LRA leadership. There has been a significant body of evidence compiled by numerous organization, particularly the Enough Project, Resolve, and Invisible Children of the LRA's presence in Kafia Kingi and South Darfur state. This detailed evidence comes from several years of interviews with ex-LRA combatants, as well as through photographic evidence, from as recent as July 2015.

The LRA's presence in Sudan, in particular of its leader Joseph Kony, creates a critical safe haven for the rebel group and allows it to traffic elephant tusks and resupply its ammunition, food, and other supplies. Simply put, the LRA would not survive if it were not for its safe havens in Sudanese-held territory. Despite this fact, the African Union Regional Task Force of the Regional Cooperation Initiative for the Elimination of the Lord's Resistance Army (RCI-LRA) has not been allowed by the Sudanese government to operate in Sudan.

- As late as July 2015, there is at least one group of LRA present in Kafia Kingi, according to recent LRA defectors.
- LRA leader Joseph Kony currently has approximately 20 armed men with him in Kafia Kingi. By April 17, 2015, Kony's group was based near Mt Toussoro (geo coordinates 9.06667, 23.23333).
- Kony has rarely left Kafia Kingi since he moved there in early 2011. He moved to CAR in March 2012 for a short period of time but returned to the same area soon after. There are more than a dozen LRA 'positions' (areas where Kony and his group camps for a night or two) in this area that we have documented.
- As of July 2015, former LRA fighters reported that Kony has instructed most fighters to not disclose his presence to anyone outside of the LRA and to tell SAF soldiers that Kony is in CAR.
- For at least the past year, one of Kony's sons, Ali, and a trusted bodyguard have engaged in trading (barter) of ivory for food, ammunition and military uniforms with two Sudanese merchants from the town of Songo. The traders bring food, ammunition and uniforms on motorcycles to prearranged rendezvous points within Kafia Kingi. They meet with one of Kony's sons or trusted bodyguard and agree on number of tusks to be bartered for their goods. Exchanges have happened as frequently as three times a month.

- A group of seven defectors who surrendered to the UPDF in June 2015 (from Kony's groups in Kafia Kingi) came out with more than 350 rounds of ammunition, indications that Kony's group has received fresh supplies of ammo.
- Garamba National Park rangers in Congo reported finding spent ammunition rounds, believed to have been shot by LRA poachers. The rounds had Arabic writings on the casings, possibly rounds issued by the Sudan Armed Forces (SAF).
- Kony is in possession of an unspecified number of elephant tusks but it is believed to be around 50 pieces with a latest consignment arriving from DRC's Garamba park in early 2015. He then buried between 20-40 pieces alongside other tusks that groups brought before, likely in the third quarter of 2014.

LRA defectors who witnessed Joseph Kony's presence in Kafia Kingi and/or South Darfur or had heard about his presence in those areas from other LRA commanders

1. LRA combatant (Kony bodyguard). Date of defection: May 2015
- Kony spent a brief period in eastern CAR in October 2014, then in November 2014 he returned to Kafia Kingi. His group has been moving frequently around the CAR/Darfur/Kafia Kingi border area, often around the Umbelacha River in Kafia Kingi.
- In March 2015, Kony ordered one of his commanders to trade between 5-10 pieces of ivory with a Songo-based Sudanese merchant. The ivory was traded for food. The ivory had been collected by LRA commander Awila from Garamba National Park in mid-2014.

2. LRA combatant (Kony bodyguard). Date of defection: May 2015
- Was operating in DR Congo and eastern CAR during 2014. In March 2015 his group traveled to Kafia Kingi, where they met with Kony's group, near the Umbelacha and Pipi Rivers. They stayed in that border area until he escaped in May 2015.

3. LRA Commander Dominic Ongwen. Date of defection: January 2015
- "Kony told me that he wanted to take me to Darfur since Odhiambo had died, and because I was the most senior commander after him. But other commanders had told me that he planned to kill me from Darfur after saying the spirit told him I and several officers wanted to defect. But when we reached Darfur, he ordered for my arrest on December 14, 2014. While in prison, I was given 250 strokes of the cane. I was tied on a rope for a week and I could only pass bloody urine. Later some LRA commanders released me."

4. Sam Ouandja, CAR: FACA/UFDR/Gendarmarie joint meeting, 24/10/12
- When Union of Democratic Forces for Unity (UFDR) forces pursued an LRA group in late 2010, the LRA were trying to cross the border into the Kafia Kingi enclave. UFDR

clashed with them at the border, allowing abductees to escape, but LRA combatants went across the border.

- People from Dafak in KK enclave (Note: Interviewees clearly distinguished Dafak from Um Dafok) cross the border and come to Sam Ouandja Some of them have said that the LRA is cultivating fields south of Dafak.
- LRA abducted some Mbororo children in April 2012 and Mbororo followed them to the Ngi River (which they placed somewhere near the Kafia Kingi/CAR border) to rescue abducted children. LRA crossed into Kafia Kingo enclave after Mbororo attacked them.

5. Sam Ouandja, CAR. Dafak "refugee" camp, 25/10/12

- LRA have a camp 2 kilometers south of Dafak. Sudanese government gave them tools and land where they could cultivate. LRA have had a presence there for three years. People travel from Dafak to Sam Ouandja in the dry season, and have seen them there.
- Collaboration between LRA and SAF is like the collaboration between the FACA and UFDR.
- LRA camp south of Dafak is at a place called Garmadora, which was actually the village that many of the interviewed people present were from…. "The LRA is living in our home village."
- LRA cultivates fields at a place called Shara-Jil, which is several km from Garmadora.
- They mentioned the LRA camp as being near the Bahar Arab River (more commonly known as Ambalacha), which they identified as the river that makes up part of the northern boundary of the Kafia Kingi enclave.
- Wives of the LRA come to the market to sell produce from their fields. They are armed and have shaved heads.

6. Raga, South Sudan. SPLA Military Intelligence

- In October/November 2011, Kony arrives in Dafak. Somewhere in this time period, SAF moves LRA camp closer to their Dafak barracks, about 8-10 kilometers southeast of the barracks. The area is very swampy and wet, with the barracks occupying a strategic high ground. A small stream divides the SAF barracks from the LRA camp. The SAF contingent is commanded by a Capt. Ali and contains 180-200 total troops.
- On 13 January 2012, LRA Lance Corporal Okot Robert Palabek is captured by SPLA southwest of Boro Madina after defecting from an LRA group in Kafia Kingi. Palabek states that SAF has given LRA uniforms and food.
- Since early 2012, LRA officers go on a "weekly" basis to Songo market with SAF escorts. Sometimes other LRA go as far as Dimbeshara and wait there. LRA presence in Songo market confirmed by human intelligence. LRA hasn't gone to market as much during rainy season.

7. Testimony of Central African male, escaped from the LRA near Nzako, CAR. He was abducted by the LRA in February 2014.

- On the last mission he participated in to retrieve ivory, they returned to a location called Pipi in CAR around late April 2015 and delivered 20 tusks to Lamola. Lamola then sent the tusks to Sudan with an escort of 30 people.
- The Séléka gave the LRA some food for free between town of Sam Ouandja and Sudan, goods like sugar and rice.
- In Sudan the LRA is happy as they have everything they need and if there is something they just ask their partners or other LRA groups to go get it.

8. Testimony of Central African male, November 2014

- Martin said that when he escaped in November 2014, his group had mostly been in CAR and DRC, however, his group was on its way to Darfur when he escaped. According to Martin, they were going to Darfur to meet Kony.

9. Testimony of 25-year-old ex-combatant from South Sudan. Escaped late October 2014.

- In September 2014, two (2) LRA groups met and he was transferred to Owela's group, which was on its way to Darfur to meet Kony and get new orders/assignments for the group.
- Aligac's group: 7 officers, 9 soldiers, 20 women
- Owela's group: 9 officers, 8 soldiers, and 12 women

10. Central African traders based in Sam Ouandja

We have received credible reports from Central African traders that indicate traders in the Sam Ouandja and Kafia Kingi region are regularly meeting with LRA groups and trading food andsupplies for ivory.

11. LRA Defector, October 2014

"Kony knows that everyone is aware that he is in Darfur [Kafia Kingi] now, so he is trying to confuse the enemy. He might leave some fighters there, but most will move into DRC to take attention away from him."

12. Community representatives in Sam Ouandja, eastern CAR, November 2014

"We know it's LRA from the way they do their "business," how they kill and abduct people. We don't know anyone else who does [it] like this. They came from the direction of southern Darfur, and the people in the group spoke different languages. Some spoke Arabic, and some spoke languages that we did not understand and had never heard before. [....] The group returned back towards Sudan."

APPENDIX A. MAP AND DETAILED TIMELINE OF REPORTED LRA ACTIVITY IN AND AROUND
THE KAFIA KINGI ENCLAVE, 2009-2013

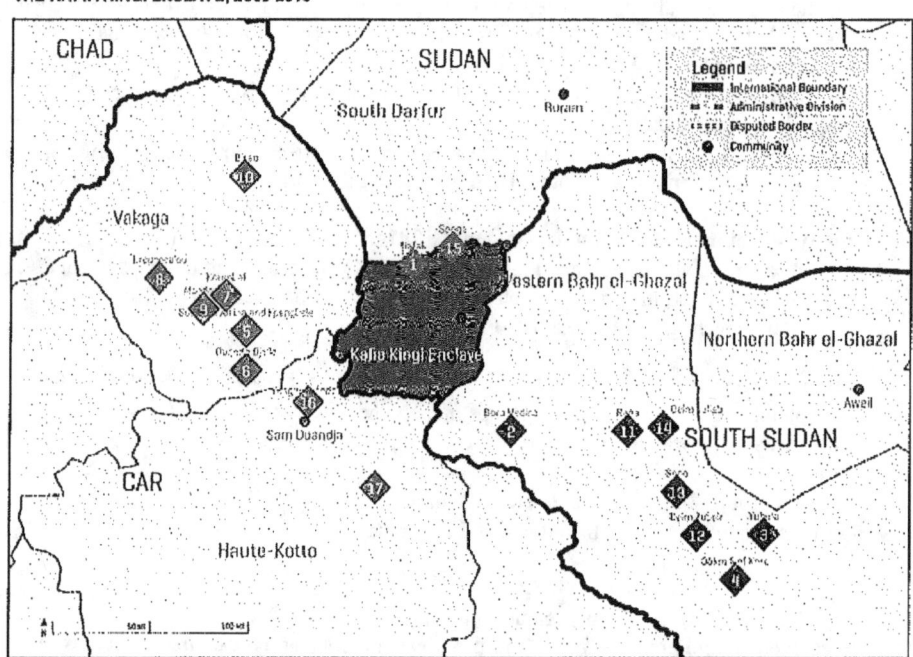

Description of the following images:
- "Index of images: • Figure 1: This satellite image from March 2012 shows where the
  LRA likely developed an encampment on the banks of the Umbelasha River,
  approximately seventeen kilometers southwest of a Sudanese military garrison within the
  Kafia Kingi enclave. © DigitalGlobe 2013 • Figure 2: This image, also from March 2012,
  zooms in on the rectangular area highlighted in Figure 1 and shows semi-permanent
  structures being built, presumably to shelter LRA members. © DigitalGlobe 2013 •
  Figure 3: The camp reached peak activity in December 2012 during harvest season. There
  are four separate areas with structures; only one central encampment features tukuls
  while the surrounding camps feature tents and other makeshift structures. © DigitalGlobe
  2013 • Figure 4: The tukuls measure 6 meters in diameter, while the smaller tent-like
  structures measure approximately 1.5 meters by 4 meters. © DigitalGlobe 2013 • Figure
  5: Side-by-side imagery from December 2012 and March 2013 shows that the camp was
  abandoned by March 2013."[1]

[1] Enough Project, Invisible Children, and The Resolve, "Hidden in Plain Sight: Sudan's Harboring of the LRA in
the Kafia Kingi Enclave, 2009-2013" (April 2013), available at
http://www.enoughproject.org/files/HiddeninPlainSight_Sudans_SupporttotheLRA_April2013.pdf.

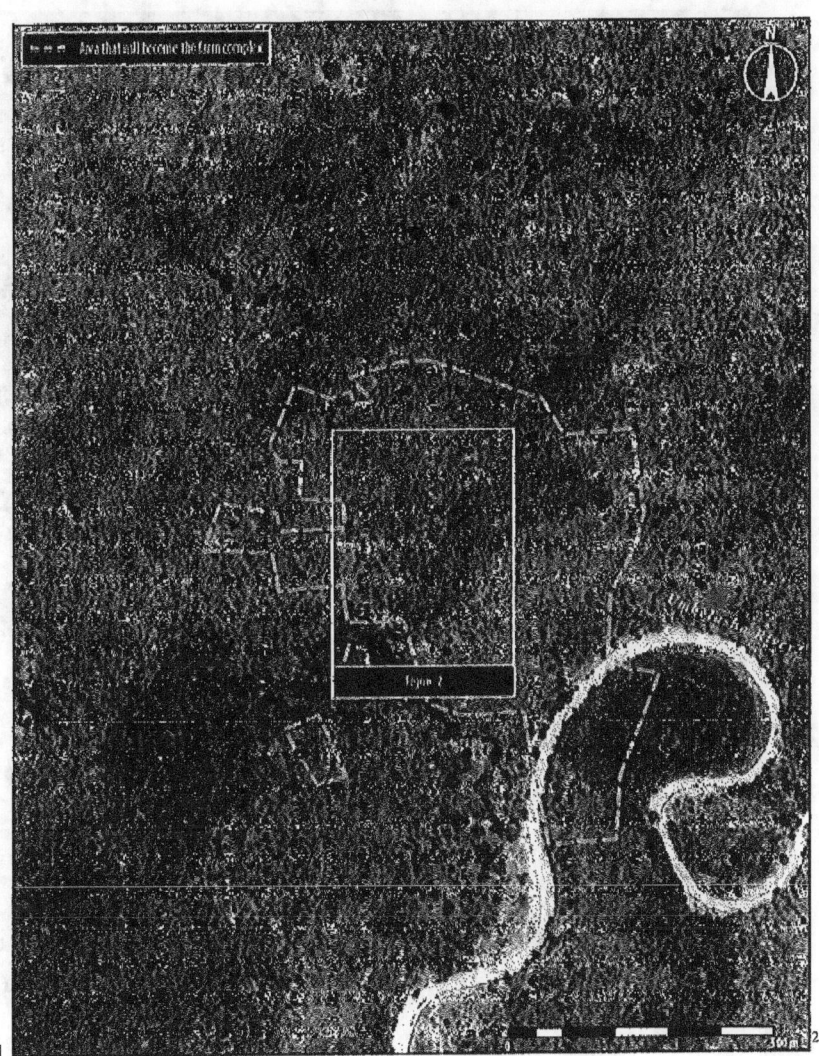

² Enough Project, Invisible Children, and The Resolve, "Hidden in Plain Sight: Sudan's Harboring of the LRA in the Kafia Kingi Enclave, 2009-2013" (April 2013), available at http://www.enoughproject.org/files/HiddenInPlainSight_Sudans_SupporttotheLRA_April2013.pdf.

[3] Enough Project, Invisible Children, and The Resolve, "Hidden in Plain Sight: Sudan's Harboring of the LRA in the Kafia Kingi Enclave, 2009-2013" (April 2013), available at http://www.enoughproject.org/files/HiddeninPlainSight_Sudans_SupporttotheLRA_April2013.pdf.

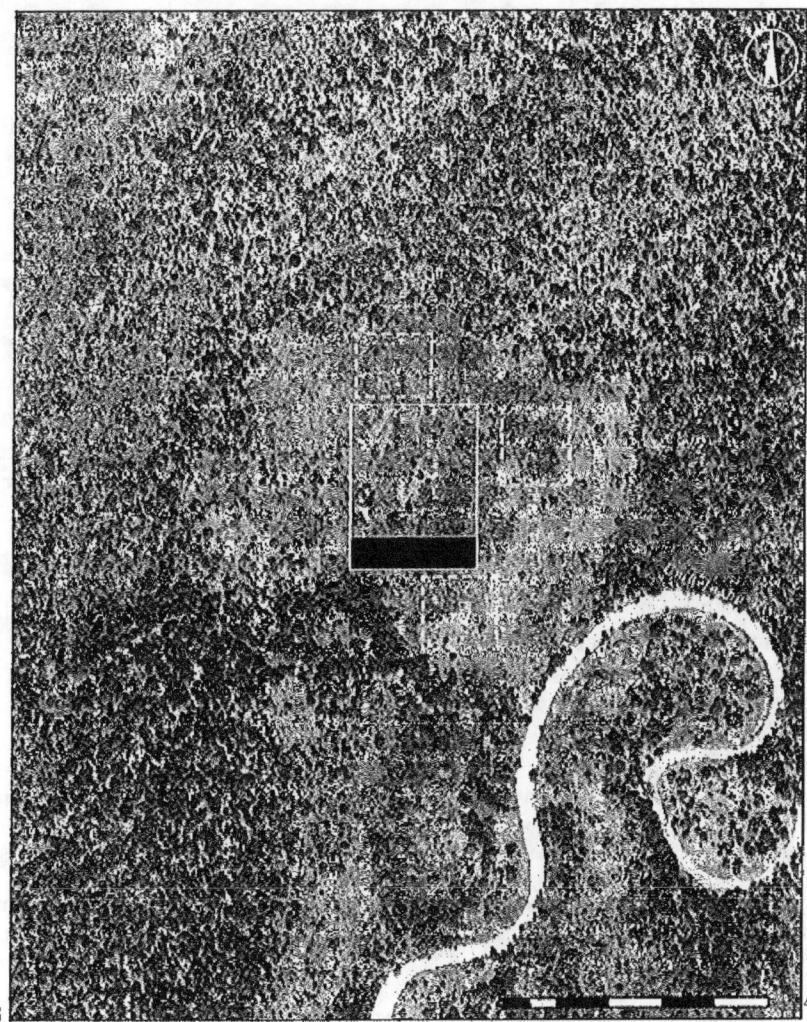

The complete version of this document can be accessed here:

http://docs.house.gov/meetings/FA/FA16/20150930/104002/HHRG-114-FA16-Wstate-LezhnevS-20150930-SD001.pdf

---

[4] Enough Project, Invisible Children, and The Resolve, "Hidden in Plain Sight: Sudan's Harboring of the LRA in the Kafia Kingi Enclave, 2009-2013" (April 2013), available at http://www.enoughproject.org/files/HiddeninPlainSight_Sudans_SupporttotheLRA_April2013.pdf.

ADDRESS BY MUHAMMADU BUHARI
PRESIDENT, FEDERAL REPUBLIC OF NIGERIA AT THE 70TH SESSION OF THE
UNITED NATIONS GENERAL ASSEMBLY,
NEW YORK, 28TH SEPTEMBER 2015.

President of the General Assembly,
Secretary–General

Your Excellencies Heads of State and Governments
Distinguished Delegates
Ladies and Gentlemen,

I would like, Mr. President, on behalf of the Government and people of Nigeria, to congratulate
you and your country on your election to preside over the 70th session of the U.N. General
Assembly.

2. May I also express appreciation to your predecessor, Mr. Sam Kahamba Kutesa and the
Secretary General Mr. Ban Ki-moon both of whom worked tirelessly to ensure proper
articulation of the post-2015 Development Agenda and to maintain the focus and commitment to
the ideals of the United Nations. I thank Mr. Ban Ki-moon for his recent visit to Nigeria when
we held very useful discussions.

Mr. President,

3. Fifty-five (55) years ago almost to the day, my great predecessor, Nigeria's first Prime
Minister, Alhaji Abubakar Tafawa Balewa stood on this forum to declare Nigeria's desire to
develop and maintain friendly relations with all countries. He also assured the world of our
country's commitment to uphold the principles upon which the United Nations was founded.

4. Mr. President, my country, Nigeria, has lived by this conviction, even when judgement went
against us in territorial disputes with our neighbours. We respected those judgements and abided
by them as a mark of respect for the rule of law and the charter of this organization. Nigeria's
record in the U.N. peacekeeping is second to none. I myself as a young officer in the Nigerian
Army did tours of duty in Congo and the Lebanon.

5. Nigeria has contributed to U.N. peacekeeping efforts in Ethiopia, Liberia, Sierra Leone and
Darfur. Furthermore, we are proud of our contributions to other activities of the U.N. including
the Peace Building Commission, the Human Rights Council and security sector reform.

Mr. President,

6. We are gratified to note that most countries have pledged commitment to the post-2015
Development Agenda and the Sustainable Development Goals (SDGs) with their means of
implementation. The successor frameworks of the MDGs have come, Mr. President, with lofty
aspirations and if I may say so, heroic assumptions! Nonetheless, they target development
cooperation by the international community up to the year 2020. And they deserve universal
support.

7. This is because the SDGs mirror the hopes and aspirations of much of the world.

8. I should stress that for the newly adopted SDGs to be truly global, they must be practical. In this regard, the SDGs' core objectives of poverty eradication and reducing inequalities must be met within the framework of a revitalized global partnership support by concrete policies and actions as outlined in the Addis Ababa Action Agenda.

9. Luckily, these two core objectives of the SDGs are precisely at the centre of Nigeria's new Administration's agenda. It must be emphasized, Mr. President, that Foreign Direct Investment supplemented where suitable by Official Development Assistance as outlined in the Addis Ababa Agenda are necessary, though not sufficient, conditions for accelerated development in countries that are trying to catch up.

10. In this connexion, I would like to appeal to industrialized countries to redeem their pledge of earmarking 0.7% (nought point seven percent) of their GDP to development assistance. With the sole exception of the UK, all concerned countries have, I am told to meet the UN requirement. But, Mr. President, with SDGs we have the opportunity to improve the lives of people not just in the developing world but in all nations.

11. The Secretary General himself has grouped the SDGs into what he calls six "essential elements" namely:

• Dignity

• Prosperity

• Justice

• Partnership

• Planet

• People

As a prerequisite to these and as we look at history and remember the terrible events that gave rise to the birth of the United Nations in 1945, I would like to propose a seventh:

• PEACE

12. Peace, Mr. President, is close to the hearts of Nigerians, as we are in the front line in the war on terror. Boko Haram's war against the people of Nigeria, Chad, Niger and Cameroon may not attract as much worldwide attention as the wars in the Middle East but the suffering is just as great and the human cost is equally high.

13. This is a war about values between progress and chaos; between democracy and the rule of law. Boko Haram celebrates violence against the weak and the innocent and deplorably, they hide behind their perverted interpretation of Islam. Boko Haram is as far away from Islam as any one can think of.

14. Many of my colleagues attending this forum would want to know how our new government intends to tackle the huge problems the government has inherited. Friends of Nigeria and foreign

investor partners will be encouraged to know that the new Government is attacking the problems we inherited head-on.

15. We intend to tackle inequalities arising from massive unemployment and previous government policies favouring a few people to the detriment of the many. We intend to emphasize quality technological education for development and lay foundation for comprehensive care of the aged, the disadvantaged and the infirm. But for now terrorism is the immediate problem.

16. Accordingly, Mr. President, Members of the General Assembly, the new Nigerian Government which I have the honour to head, moved with dispatch to put in a bold and robust strategy to defeat Boko Haram. Nigeria and her neighbours Cameroon, Chad and Niger plus Benin are working together to face this common threat within the regional framework of the Lake Chad Basin Commission. We have established a multinational joint task force to confront, degrade and defeat Boko Haram.

17. We have driven them away from many of their strongholds, killed or captured many of their operatives or commanders and freed several hundreds of hostages.

18. Mr. President, one of our major aims is to rescue the Chibok girls alive and unharmed. We are working round the clock to ensure their safety and eventual reunion with their families. Chibok girls are constantly on our minds and in our plans.

19. Mr. President, terrorism is by no means the major or the only evil threatening and undermining the wellbeing of societies around the world.

• Corruption

• Cross border financial crimes

• Cyber crimes

• Human trafficking

• Spread of communicable diseases

• Climate change

• Proliferation of weapons

are all major challenges of the 21st century which the international community must tackle collectively. Let me reaffirm Nigerian government's unwavering commitment to fight corruption and illicit financial flows. By any consideration, corruption and cross border financial crimes are impediments to development, economic growth, and the realization of the wellbeing of citizens across the globe.

20. Nigeria is ready and willing to partner with international agencies and individual countries on a bilateral basis to confront crimes and corruption. In particular, I call upon the global community to urgently redouble efforts towards strengthening the mechanisms for dismantling

safe havens for proceeds of corruption and ensuring the return of stolen funds and assets to their countries of origin.

21. Mr. President, the world is now facing a big new challenge: human trafficking. This is an old evil taking an altogether new and dangerous dimension threatening to upset international relationships. We in Africa are grieved to see on international networks how hundreds of thousands of our able bodied men and women fleeing to Europe and in the process thousands dying in the desert or drowning in the Mediterranean.

22. We condemn in the strongest terms these people traffickers and will support any measures to apprehend and bring them to justice. At the same time, we are very appreciative of European governments notably Italy and Germany, for their understanding and humane treatment of these refugees.

23. Last year, our continent faced the dreadful occurrence of Ebola. We sincerely thank the international community for the collective efforts to contain this deadly disease. We are not out of the woods yet but we would like to record our appreciation to the United States, United Kingdom, France and China for their outstanding assistance in arresting the spread of Ebola and care of those infected in collaboration with host countries.

Mr. President,

24. Nigeria fully subscribes to and fully endorses Goals 13, 14 and 15 of the SDGs regarding Climate Change. In Nigeria, desertification and land erosion and degradation leading to biodiversity loss are real threats to our environment and we shall propose under the auspices of the Lake Chad Basin Commission a regional approach to combat these environmental challenges.

25. We look forward to the UN Summit on climate change in Paris in December 2015. This summit should provide optimism to humanity on addressing the looming threat faced by many communities around the world.

Mr. President,

26. We are witnessing a dreadful increase in conflicts fuelled by availability of small arms and light weapons. I call upon all member countries to demonstrate the political will needed to uphold the UN charter. For a start, a robust implementation of the Arms Trade Treaty will guarantee that small arms and light weapons are only legally transferred. Arms traffickers and human traffickers are two evil species which the world community should eradicate.

Mr. President,

27. As we engage in these annual debates, we need remind ourselves of the principles that led to the founding of the United Nations. Among those are peaceful coexistence and self-determination of peoples. In this context, Mr. President, the unresolved question of self-determination for the Palestinian people and those of Western Sahara, both nations having been adjusted by the United Nations as qualifying for this inalienable right must now be assured and fulfilled without any further delay or obstacle.

28. The international community has come to pin its hopes on resolving the Palestinian issue through the two – states solution which recognises the legitimate right of each state to exist in peace and security. The world has no more excuses or reasons to delay the implementation of the long list of Security Council resolutions on this question. Neither do we have the moral right to deny any people their freedom or condemn them indefinitely to occupation and blockade

Mr. President, delegates of member countries,

29. UN is 70 years old. It can count many more than 70 major achievements as the world's forum and family reunion. It is my hope that in the next 70 years, it will achieve control of climate, help to eliminate communicable diseases, eliminate major and local conflicts and therefore eliminate the problem of refugees, take major steps towards reducing harmful inequalities between nations and within nations and above all, eliminate nuclear weapons.

30. Mr. President, as this is my first address in this Assembly, I thank you and the delegates for listening so patiently

www.ingramcontent.com/pod-product-compliance
Lightning Source LLC
Chambersburg PA
CBHW081114280526
45787CB00007B/2826